Sam Shepard's Metaphorical Stages

Recent Titles in
Contributions in Drama and Theatre Studies
Series Editor: Joseph Donohue

A Whirlwind in Dublin: *The Plough and the Stars* Riots
Robert G. Lowery, editor

German Actors of the Eighteenth and Nineteenth Centuries: Idealism,
Romanticism, and Realism
Simon Williams

William Archer On Ibsen: The Major Essays, 1889–1919
Thomas Postlewait, editor

Theatre for Working-Class Audiences in the United States, 1830–1980
Bruce A. McConachie and Daniel Friedman, editors

Hamlet on Stage: The Great Tradition
John A. Mills

America's Musical Stage: Two Hundred Years of Musical Theatre
Julian Mates

From Farce to Metadrama: A Stage History of *The Taming of the Shrew*,
1594–1983
Tori Haring-Smith

Prophet of the New Drama: William Archer and the Ibsen Campaign
Thomas Postlewait

The Theatre of Meyerhold and Brecht
Katherine Bliss Eaton

Ten Seasons: New York Theatre in the Seventies
Samuel L. Leiter

Sam Shepard's Metaphorical Stages

LYNDA HART

CONTRIBUTIONS IN DRAMA AND THEATRE STUDIES,
NUMBER 22

Greenwood Press

NEW YORK
WESTPORT, CONNECTICUT
LONDON

Library of Congress Cataloging-in-Publication Data

Hart, Lynda, 1953–
  Sam Shepard's metaphorical stages.

  (Contributions in drama and theatre studies,
ISSN 0163-3821 ; no. 22)
  Bibliography: p.
  Includes index.
  1. Shepard, Sam, 1943–   —Criticism and
interpretation. I. Title. II. Series.
  PS3569.H394Z69   1987   812'.54   86-4616
  ISBN 0-313-25373-0 (lib. bdg. : alk. paper)

Library of Congress Catalog Card Number: 86-4616
ISBN: 0-313-25373-0
ISSN: 0163-3821

First published in 1987

Greenwood Press, Inc.
88 Post Road West, Westport, Connecticut 06881

Printed in the United States of America

∞™

The paper used in this book complies with the
Permanent Paper Standard issued by the National
Information Standards Organization (Z39.48-1984).

10 9 8 7 6 5 4 3 2 1

Copyright Acknowledgments

The author gratefully acknowledges permission to use the following:
From the Introduction by Richard Gilman to *Seven Plays* by Sam Shepard. Introduction copyright © 1981 by Bantam Books, Inc. Reprinted by permission
of the publisher. All rights reserved.
From "La Turista," "Curse of the Starving Class," "Buried Child," and "True
West," appearing in the collection *Seven Plays* by Sam Shepard. Copyrights ©
1968, 1976, 1979, and 1981 by Sam Shepard. Reprinted by permission of Bantam Books, Inc. All rights reserved. (Covering the distribution rights in the
United States, its dependencies, Canada, the Philippines, and the Open Mar-
ket throughout the world, excluding the British Commonwealth.) Reprinted by
permission of Faber & Faber Ltd. (Covering non-exclusive rights throughout
the British Commonwealth.)

In memory of my mother, and for my father

CONTENTS

ACKNOWLEDGMENTS

I would like to thank the following people for their influence, encouragement, and support: my earliest readers of the manuscript, Philip Bollier, Larry Simmons, and Edward Partridge made many fine suggestions and patiently helped me through the writing process in its first phases. Milly Barranger gave me inspiration, careful guidance, and valuable editorial assistance. Susan Krantz, Dusky Loebel, Georgeann Murphy, Sandra Stephan, and Debra Young advised and supported me with essential caring. Alice Voros's tremendous patience and understanding gave me strength through many long afternoons.

David Mayer gave me confidence, good critical advice, and an opportunity to pursue my ideas in a stimulating setting. My colleagues in the English department at Xavier University believed in the book's realization since I joined them in the Fall of 1984; I gratefully acknowledge all of their support, especially that of Ernie Fontana whose enthusiasm has been boundless. Joseph Donohue's critical insight and his careful, detailed editing of the manuscript made this book possible. Millie Gillespie and Lynda Simon patiently and expertly typed the many versions of the book.

Mary DeShazer, Catherine Keller, and Leslie Thrope have shaped and developed my life and my work in ways for which I am inexpressibly thankful; their nurturing energies have sustained me through the past two years. My family is a constant source of confidence and comfort.

Sam Shepard's
Metaphorical Stages

I

INTRODUCTION

As privately as his growing audience will allow him, Sam Shepard continues a personal quest that began twenty-two years ago in a tiny New York City apartment. For Shepard the theatre has become "a home where [he] brings the adventures of [his] life and sorts them out, making sense or non-sense out of mysterious impressions."[1] Language itself, a primary though not sole medium for the playwright, is often an obstacle in his search, "a veil hiding demons and angels which the characters are always out of touch with."[2] Those angels and demons reside in the "territories within us that are totally unknown."[3] With a fearlessness akin to innocence, Shepard delves into those terrifying regions and calls up images for the stage that speak to us from the relative safety of our auditorium seats. The "playwright as shaman," Jack Gelber has called him.[4] Shepard tries "to go into parts of [himself] that are unknown," and believes that those parts "are related to everybody."[5] He writes not to purge but to confront.

As Richard Gilman points out in his introduction to *Sam Shepard: Seven Plays*, Shepard's drama is particularly difficult to classify, a characteristic that is at once a source of our perpetual fascination with his work and a problem for critics who would like to arrange his work in a neat system. Shepard is as wily as his character Lee in *True West*. Just when we think that he might be pinned down, he is likely to spring agilely back to his feet and bar a tidy exit. Gilman finds Shepard's drama superbly resistant to conceptualization or categorization:

More than that of any important playwright I know, Shepard's work resists division into periods, stages of growth or development (with the exception of the later plays, which "seem to constitute a rough phase"). Unlike the serial way in which we arrange most writers' work in our minds, Shepard's writing seems present to us all at once, lying rudely sprawled across our consciousness.[6]

Gilman captures precisely the reader or spectator's experience of the Shepard canon. I would like to suggest, however, that Shepard's eclecticism notwithstanding, we can connect his drama to recognizable tradition. A majority of the criticism of Shepard's work is impressionistic, rather than analytic, and perpetuates diffusive readings of the plays. A number of fine articles on the individual plays establishes their coherency in isolation, but none of them offer a sustained analysis of Shepard's growth and development as a playwright. The critics have also neglected to found Shepard's plays in a dramatic tradition. Gilman's comment that the "very rootlessness of Shepard's theatre, its springing so largely from a condition outside the continuity of the stage, is a source of the difficulty we have with it,"[7] addresses the absence of critical frames of reference that would allow us entry into Shepard's drama.   In his review of *Fool for Love*, Walter Kerr asserts that Shepard either cannot or will not write plays that are accessible to a wide audience, and concludes that Shepard is a cult artist whose drama appeals to a coterie audience that possesses some mysterious communion with the playwright.[8]

This study has grown out of a desire to offer a coherent, unified vision of Shepard's drama. In the chapters that follow I hope to dispel the notion that Shepard's theatre is rootless, and dispense with the idea that Shepard emerged *sui generis*. The dramatic theories and practices of the great European innovators, Brecht, Pirandello, Artaud, Ionesco, and Beckett among them, offer a unique combination of anti-illusionistic and anti-literary methods that provide the intellectual background and lay the groundwork for the American avant-garde dramatists of the late 1950's and early 1960's. Among American theatre artists, two groups, the Living Theatre and the Open Theatre, demand attention as innovative extenders of their European forerunners' methods. While it would be impossible to establish firmly all of the theatre artists whose work has influenced the aesthetic of Shepard's drama, the European dramatists and the two American theatre groups provide a necessary and sufficient background for a study of Shepard's plays.

I have chosen ten of Shepard's plays to examine chronologically. Together they exhibit a recognizable organic development and demonstrate the efforts of a young playwright growing into maturity as he experiments with a variety of dramatic modes in search of a form that ably expresses an imaginative content. In addition to the critical survey of the plays, I have provided a career chronology, an appendix of editions and premiere productions, and a secondary bibliography.

Shepard's drama begins with the basic question "What is drama?" and the subject matter of his earliest work is self-reflexive. *Cowboys #2* (a 1967 rewrite of the lost 1964 original) is a play about the theatre that investigates the limits and possibilities of role-playing. This first play is contained within a structure that is limited and ultimately self-annihilating. In *Chicago* (1966) Shepard moves one step beyond the nihilism of total self-consciousness and creates an autonomous character whose consciousness controls, directs, and finally consumes the action of the play. The personal expressionism of *Chicago* expands to include a recognizable social world in *La Turista* (1967), a play that comments covertly on the world outside the theatre. In the social expressionistic form, Shepard continues his criticism of American society in *The Tooth of Crime* (1972), a play with mythic resonance and a classical structure. In *Action* (1975) the expressionistic method of the early plays culminates in an absurdist vision that becomes a turning point in Shepard's art.

In 1976 with *Curse of the Starving Class*, Shepard adopts a modified realism, the form that has historically been most conducive to the exploration of familial themes. *Buried Child* (1978), *True West* (1981), and *Fool for Love* (1983) followed *Curse of the Starving Class*, forming a quartet of domestic dramas, all essentially in the realistic mode. *A Lie of the Mind* (November 1985) is Shepard's epic domestic drama, a vast endeavor to crystallize the themes and action of nearly ten years of familial psychological exploration.

In the history of modern drama, we think more often in terms
of movements than genres. The two most important movements in modern drama, serious naturalism and psychological
expressionism, have continued to exist side by side in the contemporary theatre. Critics of the American drama began to de-
cry naturalism in the late 1950's when an increasing number of
American practitioners were mechanically borrowing the realistic conventions of naturalism without genuinely reflecting on
their usefulness in representing contemporary thought. As late
as 1963, in reference to the European drama, Richard Gilman
complained: "We still do not understand what they are about;
and we go on believing that we can effect our regeneration
without such understanding."[9]

Raymond Williams points out that serious naturalism and
psychological expressionism do not really posit conflicting claims.
Although the conventions differ, both are inherently critical
forms: naturalism dramatizes "a tension which still drew much
of its force from the physical existence of an unacceptable world,
and from the presence in it of others, in the same dimension,
with whom the attempt at a common understanding . . . must
continue to be made"; expressionism dramatizes "a related tension which remade the world and its persons in its own terms:
not for liberation from it—but to show what it really was; to
expose it."[10]

Shepard's early plays are variations of expressionism; they
have in common dramatic actions that are efforts to remake the
world or create it anew in a personal vision. The gradual movement toward social commentary builds into a confrontation with
the unacceptable world as Shepard's drama becomes increasingly naturalistic. The fantastic unlocalized settings in the early
plays become middle-class American homes in the later plays,
but similar illusions hold though they are played and experienced differently. In the last scene of *Action*, the play that marks
the end of Shepard's expressionistic period, Jeep's final words
are: "No escape, that's it, no escape."[11] For the characters in
Shepard's early plays, there is no liberation; their exits are as
theatrical and unrealistic as Kent's final leap through the upstage wall in *La Turista*. In the naturalistic plays, Shepard's
families exist in a community that was only a vague memory

for the characters in *Action*; and though they are equally trapped, socially and psychologically determined as they struggle against the continuity thrust upon them by inheritance, they are seeking liberation from their unacceptable worlds.
— From Shepard's first highly self-conscious dramatic efforts he follows a natural development through a variety of forms—personal expressionism, social expressionism, and absurdism, at the last returning to a modified realism, the dramatic form that heralded the beginning of modern drama. Although he reverses the historical order in the tradition, Shepard's dramatic career nevertheless recapitulates the major movements in the drama of the twentieth century. —

NOTES

1. Sam Shepard, as quoted by Rudy Cohn in *Contemporary Dramatists*, 2nd ed., ed. James Vinson (New York: St. Martin's Press, 1977), p. 722.
2. Ibid.
3. Sam Shepard, as quoted by John Lion, "Rock 'n Roll Jesus with a Cowboy Mouth: Sam Shepard is the Inkblot of the '80s," *American Theatre*, 1, No. 1 (April 1984), p. 12.
4. Jack Gelber, "The Playwright as Shaman," in *American Dreams: The Imagination of Sam Shepard*, ed. Bonnie Marranca (New York: Performing Arts Journal Press, 1981), p. 45.
5. Lion, p. 12.
6. Richard Gilman, introduction, *Sam Shepard: Seven Plays* (New York: Bantam Books, 1981), p. xv.
7. Ibid., p. xx.
8. Walter Kerr, "Where Has Sam Shepard Led His Audience?" *New York Times*, 5 June 1983, sec. 2, p. 1, 16.
9. Richard Gilman, "The Drama is Coming Now," in *The Modern American Theatre: A Collection of Critical Essays*, ed. Alvin B. Kernan (Englewood Cliffs, N.J.: Prentice-Hall Inc., 1967), p. 158.
10. Raymond Williams, *Drama from Ibsen to Brecht* (New York: Penguin Books, 1981), pp. 392–393.
11. Sam Shepard, *Action* in *Action and the Unseen Hand* (London: Faber and Faber, 1975), p. 38. Subsequent references to this edition will be cited in the text.

II

MODEST BEGINNINGS

In 1963 Sam Shepard left southern California to tour with the Bishop's Repertory Company, a theatrical troupe that traveled the United States presenting dramatic adaptations of novels and Christian-oriented dramas. When the group stopped in New York City, Shepard got off the bus and decided to stay. After wandering around the city for a few days, Shepard looked up an old high-school friend, Charles Mingus Jr., who gave him a place to stay on the Lower East Side and helped him find a job as a busboy at the Village Gate. Unknown to Shepard, a revolution was quietly gathering force in the cellars, lofts, churches, and cafes of the surrounding neighborhood, a revolution he would soon join to become one of its major spokesmen.

The early 1960's were desperate years for the American theatre. Nineteen sixty-three marked the beginning of a decade that John Simon aptly labeled *Uneasy Stages* in his 1975 chronicle of the New York stage. In his introduction Simon speaks of "the desperate condition" of Broadway theatre, which was "not the American theatre, of course, still less the theatre *tout court*."[1] Even so, Simon acknowledged Broadway's centrality and expressed uncertain faith that its decline would benefit the future of peripheral theatre. Speculating on the theatre of the future, Simon believed that it would have to undergo a radical transformation into "an elitist art form":

It may have to give up competing with film in the grandioseness of its *mise en scène*, with television in its undemanding frivolity, with rock music and lyrics in their simple-minded accessibility.[2]

Robert Brustein's *Seasons of Discontent* bears further witness to the general critical uneasiness about the state of the theatre arts in the years when Off-Off-Broadway was quietly germinating. Brustein recorded his dramatic opinions of the theatre in the years 1959–1965. His discontent is evident as he rails against the American theatre that had fallen into "the hands of spoilers and profiteers," resulting in "one style [conventional realism] dominat[ing] our stage, and one system of acting [the Stanislavski method]; plays [having] lost their relevance to the deeper realities of contemporary life."[3]

A major cause of the deplorable status of the American theatre in the late 1950's and early 1960's could be attributed to the economic superstructures that controlled Broadway productions. The commercial theatre depended on profits obtained by dramatic art that failed to question pat moralities or challenge existing forms. A similar condition had existed in the American theatre at the turn of this century when the long-run hit was the primary goal of a New York theatre governed by a powerful group of booking agents, theatre owners, and producers. These mighty syndicates bankrupted competing theatres and favored the "star system" over ensemble acting. In reaction against the New York commercial monopoly and in response to the independent theatres of Europe, America's "little theatres" had sprung up first in New York and then all over the country. Depending on volunteers and donations, groups like the Provincetown Players, the Washington Square Players, the Chicago Little Theatre, and the Toy Theatre had begun imitating the dramatic practices of the European innovators and providing opportunities for new theatre artists to develop and refine their craft. It was out of the little theatre movement that the modern American theatre was born.

The birth of the contemporary American theatre was similarly generated. Though less widespread than the little theatre movement in the first two decades of this century, the burgeoning of Off-Off-Broadway may in reflection prove to be as significant an event. Off-Off-Broadway found its modest beginnings in Joe Cino's little storefront cafe where two new plays by fledgling playwrights were offered each evening in an intimate, relaxed atmosphere. Following Cino's initiative in 1958,

Al Carmines began producing plays in the choir loft of Judson's Memorial Church in 1961. And Ellen Stewart borrowed
profits from her bathing suit manufacturing company to open
La Mama Experimental Theatre Club, another modified cafe
where patrons could see new plays for the price of a cup of
coffee or tea. Edward Albee and his producers backed the Playwrights' Unit, which allowed new playwrights to produce their
work for a select audience. In 1964, Michael Allen founded the
arts program at the Episcopalian St. Mark's Church in-the-
Bouwerie where Ralph Cook organized Theatre Genesis in the
parish hall. In the evenings Cook was headwaiter at the Village
Gate, and his enthusiasm for his new project at St. Mark's caught
the attention of a young busboy, Sam Shepard, whose first two
plays, *Cowboys* and *The Rock Garden* appeared on Theatre Genesis's first bill. Michael Smith of *The Village Voice* attended the
opening and drew attention to Shepard's promise. Later he
would cite "the discovery of Shepard as (Theatre Genesis's)
major achievement to date."[4] Smith defined the geography of
Off-Off-Broadway: "Four places—one cafe, one theatre club, two
churches—provide space and sponsorship for most of the current projects."[5]

The artistic boundaries, however, were not so easily defined.
A new frontier had opened up for artists devoted to the revi-
talization of the American theatre, and its range and potential
seemed limitless. Unlike Off-Broadway, which began with similar intentions but quickly succumbed to high rents and the demand for commercial success, Off-Off-Broadway held fast to
the idea of theatre as "an alternative to the established theatre
rather than a way into it."[6] In 1967, Robert J. Schroeder edited
one of the first collections of plays by America's new playwrights. His hyperbolic description of the Off-Off-Broadway
movement as "quite as revolutionary an anti-doctrine as the
post-Renaissance Western mind (could) conceive," nevertheless captures the spirited enthusiasm of its members.[7] Empha-
sizing the radical nature of the new dramaturgy, Schroeder called
it "underground theatre" that "defies all traditionalism and
training."[8]

No doctrine defined the work of the Off-Off-Broadway artists; no dramaturgical method or theory alone could account

for the enormous variety of dramatic structures that were produced in this energetically creative period. While the established theatre continued to rely on the principles of the well-
made play, the Off-Off-Broadway artists were experimenting
with a variety of techniques aimed at freeing the stage from
rigid conventions. Schroeder's representative collection includes Murray Mednick's *Sand* and Sam Shepard's *Red Cross*,
both based on "manic monologues" in which "their characters
take turns in spinning intriguing whirls of imaginative fancy in
obsessively incongruous circumstances"; Ronald Tavel's *The Life
of Lady Godiva*, Maria Irene Fornes's *Promenade* and Rochelle
Owen's *Istanboul*, three plays that "comment on the sociologi-
cal and psychological situation of twentieth-century Americans
in terms of movie-derived fantasy"; Tom Sankey's *The Golden
Screw*, which "juxtaposes surrealistic musical commentary in a
rock-and-roll vein with vaudeville-type blackout scenes"; and
Jean Claude van Itallie's *I'm Really Here*, a "fantasy portrait of
the tragic end product of the American dream."[9]

Sam Shepard would employ similar methods throughout his
work. Like *Red Cross* (1966), *Icarus' Mother* (1965) and *La Turista*
(1967) depend heavily on the use of "manic monologues" and
"induce a feeling of jarring disorientation like the wiggles and
dazzles of op art" as they seek dramatic expression of "the bizarre irrational reaches of human expression."[10] *The Mad Dog
Blues* (1971), subtitled a "two-act adventure show," is a fantasy
drama in which famous film stars and mythical figures move
freely through time and space. In *The Tooth of Crime* (1972) and
Suicide in B^b (1976) Shepard uses rock-and-roll and jazz respec-
tively to comment on the action of the play. The importance
of vaudeville-derived techniques in Shepard's drama can be
detected as early as *Cowboys #2* (1967) and as late as *True
West* (1981). The tragic demise of the American dream in five
succeeding phases becomes Shepard's obsessive subject in his
domestic plays. Although no single theory bound the Off-
Off-Broadway playwrights together, they shared a common
dedication to saving the American theatre from intellectual stag-
nation. They saw themselves as on the brink of great new discov-
eries and ardently worked to create theatrical environments and
dramatic forms that could freely explore the social unrest, moral

ambiguity, and political upheaval of the decade. A strong communal bond was thus established among the initiates.

Ralph Cook described the thrust and purpose of the new movement:

The result of what we and the other theatres are doing is revolutionary. We are creating a truly indigenous theatre. The actors, directors, and writers are members of a geographical community and are presenting plays for members of that community, not as a special gala event, but as an integral everyday part of the life of the community.[11]

The tone adopted to describe the new theatre was often charged with religious fervor, as in Cook's exclamatory: "Here now, in lower Manhattan the phenomenon is taking place: the beginning, the Genesis, of a cultural revolution."[12] Schroeder found in Shepard's play a voice particularly suited to spiritual rebirth: "Shepard asks his audience to shake off its preconceptions and stereotypic reactions. Like a New Testament preacher, he pleads for a recovery of innocence and a spiritual rebirth."[13]

The Reverend Al Carmines of Judson's Memorial Church recognized an important bond between the church, the community, and the artist, whom he viewed as a "secular prophet in the city."[14] Discounting any intrinsic relationship between the messages of the church and those of the theatre it fostered, Carmines nevertheless saw a connection between the church and the theatre in their mutual desire to serve and enlighten the public in a medium freed from the condescension and distrust of the commercial theatre. Ellen Stewart also expressed the zealous mission of the new theatre:

The artist has always been the prophet of mankind, and it is evident in the writings of the new playwrights that society for its survival must become oriented to exercising its imagination to the utmost. That is exactly what the new playwrights are doing.[15]

Richard Gilman has said that Shepard appears to have emerged "precisely from the breakdown or absence—on the level of art if not of commerce—of all such traditions in America."[16] In their own territory, circumscribed by the limiting dramatic theories and methods practiced in America, Shepard and his contemporaries seemed to overthrow or defy all existing forms and conventions. The Off-Off-Broadway artists were thus bound together by their anti-traditional stance; and, like all avant-garde movements, their revolution arose from a common need to reassess the purpose and direction of art and, indeed, to redefine the theatre as a medium.

Robert Brustein had grave misgivings about the seriousness of the contemporary avant-garde in the years 1969 to 1974. He found the "bewildering parade of movements" that included happenings, camp theatre, theatre of the ridiculous, guerrilla theatre, and street theatre "less a record of permanent achievement than a record of historical change, amazing us more with the fickleness of taste than with much impression of artistic power."[17] What he found most lacking was "the development of an artistic consciousness, either in the practitioner or the spectator."[18] But later in the same collection of essays, Brustein admits that the talent which grew up during this period (and never before, he concedes, had there been such a large number of young writers with serious ambitions) had in common "the search for an authentic poetic vision."[19] Sam Shepard's is the first name on Brustein's list of these dedicated new artists.

Shepard and his contemporaries were at the forefront of one of those moments in the dialectical history of drama that Eugène Ionesco has described as "the will to renewal" for any generation of revolutionary artists:

Every movement, every fresh generation, introduces a new style or tries to do so, because the artists are clearly or dimly aware that a particular way of saying things is worn out and that a new way must be sought; or that the old exhausted idiom, the old forms, must be exploded, because they have grown incapable of containing the new things that have to be said.[20]

Then it is, he adds, that we first notice the innovation, the distinction between the works and traditional forms that preceded them. As their newness wears off, however, it is "above all their resemblance with much older works and a certain common identity that may be most noticeable."[21]

Soon after Shepard's work began to claim critical attention, quite naturally his reviewers focused on the novel aspect in his plays. It is important, however, to recognize the bond that unites his drama with the Western tradition; for it is this commonality, together with his unique and individual talent, that has allowed Shepard's work to endure and develop. Shepard's drama begins with the retreat from realism that characterized the American stage in the 1960's. In this historical and aesthetic context, his art speaks in harmony with the contemporary artists of the decade.

Schroeder notices in his introduction to *The New Underground Theatre* that the representative plays of the period have in common a rejection of naturalism. But the naturalism they rejected was merely a set of conventions; for it was, above all, an attempt to recapture reality that motivated their efforts. Robbe-Grillet points out that all literary revolutions are made in the name of realism:

out of a concern for realism each new literary school has sought to destroy the one which preceded it. . . . When a form of writing has lost its initial vitality, its force, its violence, when it has become a vulgar recipe, an academic mannerism which its followers respect only out of routine or laziness . . . then it is indeed a return to the real which constitutes the arraignment of the dead formulas and the search for new forms capable of continuing the effort.[22]

As we might have expected, then, one of the first targets for the new dramatists was the "illusion of reality"—the dramatic effect aimed for by fourth wall, proscenium-arch theatre. The attack on the fourth wall convention, however, was not simply a matter of altering the physical space where the drama takes place, but a radical revisioning of dramatic art. Robert Brustein partially agreed with critics who blamed the staleness of American theatre on the picture-frame stage: "that it 'boxes a performance in' (Atkinson), that it tends to force the playwright into 'contriving, curtailing, and distorting' (Kerr), and that it sometimes 'fixes and narrows the action to one moment in time and space' (Wilder)."[23] But in the last analysis, Brustein concludes that "the determination of the dramatist to confront or evade a specific problem is a question of conscience and vision and has almost nothing to do with the stage for which he writes."[24] Although the well-made play as a form was perpetuated by proscenium-arch sets, Richard Gilman identified the crucial barrier to authentic vision, the idea of a play as "a structure in which to trap, shape, control, exemplify, and give significance to the major passions or to their perversions, which we further expect to embody themselves in the form of characters who will then work out their destinies along the unreeling line of plot."[25] The lofts, cellars, and cafes of Off-Off-Broadway were new spaces that discouraged audiences from viewing plays as fixed, determinate, closed structures. The new playwrights of America were questioning traditional concepts of plot and character. The whole idea of human action and interaction, and thus the nature of dramatic art, was reopened for investigation.

In the history of the American drama, there was no real precedent for such a radical revision. But on the continent, such major innovators as Luigi Pirandello, Antonin Artaud, Bertolt Brecht, Eugène Ionesco, and Samuel Beckett had laid the foundation that would free the American playwrights from inherited rigidities by offering them alternate models and theories. The pathway to renewal was marked by a dramatic self-consciousness, a questioning of the very nature of theatre, and thus the exploration turned inward. According to Gilman, "This questioning is what fixes 'modern art,' and most radically separates it from what came before."[26] The key to the new theatre was the self-consciousness of the artist; the new forms were thus self-reflexive, calling attention to themselves as artifice.

In the drama, Lionel Abel seems to be the first critic to use the term "metatheatre" in a full-length discussion of the self-conscious theatre.[27] Recently, June Schlueter has studied extensively the metafictional character in the drama of Pirandello, Genet, Beckett, Weiss, Albee, Stoppard, and Handke.[28] Shepard's early plays are distinctly metatheatrical, yet he expresses very little sense of tradition. He was only nineteen when he wrote his first two plays and had little formal education. With one playwriting attempt behind him, a self-acknowledged bad imitation of a Tennessee Williams play,[29] Shepard arrived in New York with few preconceptions about the nature of drama.

He remembers a beatnik at a party dropping a copy of *Waiting for Godot* in his lap. He read it, but "didn't know anything about what it *was*."[30] He mentioned Brecht as his favorite playwright. He respects the abstract expressionism of Jackson Pollock and admires the theatrical experiments of Peter Brook. He vaguely remembers seeing an Albee play shortly after he arrived in New York. Shepard's taciturnity has frustrated critics. Gilman suspects Shepard of "wanting to be thought *sui generis*, a self-creation."[31] Michael Smith, the first critic to recognize Shepard's promise, found Shepard's voice "distinctly American and his own," but was certain that Shepard had been aware of European models.[32]

We do know that the self-consciousness of the artist as subject for dramatic expression was widespread on the New York stage in the early 1960's. In the spring of 1963, Off-Broadway offered Pinter's *The Collection*, a play in which the central dramatic question is never answered. On the same bill, *The Dumb Waiter* presented characters whose actions are controlled by some mysterious offstage presence, like actors who are trying frantically to improvise a half-remembered script. The Martinique Theatre revived Pirandello's *Six Characters in Search of an Author*, the play that established the theoretical foundations of metatheatre and, in one reviewer's words, is a "magnificent imaging of the theatre: its magic, callousness, and disturbing dual citizenship in fact and dream. . . . "[33] In the winter of 1963, Anouilh's *The Rehearsal* was imported to New York from London, another play-within-a-play that emphasizes the theatricality of action. In the summer of 1964, John Gielgud directed *Hamlet* in an apparent Pirandellian revision since the actors (not in "The Mousetrap" but in *Hamlet*) were dressed as if in dress rehearsal. In the spring of 1964, Alan Schneider brought Beckett's *Play* to the Cherry Lane.

Whether or not Shepard actually attended any of these productions, it is scarcely possible that he could have avoided the impact of metatheatre when even the mainstream theatres were beginning to concentrate on plays that called attention to themselves as artifice. The stage, no longer mirroring the world, was beginning to reflect its own image as the highly self-conscious playwright used the stage as a metaphor for consciousness. Mi-

mesis, as not only method, but subject, was becoming firmly
established as viable content for drama on the American stage.
The theories and practices of the great European innovators
were at last gaining a stronghold in the American theatre. Pirandello's dramatic situations opened up endless possibilities for
the daring exploration of the interplay between life and art,
fluidity and form. His excavations into the nature of the theatrical illusion recovered for future playwrights the drama's ability to use the medium for examination of the creative process.
Artaud's theoretical writings helped shape the course of the
American avant-garde theatre in the 1960's by radically calling
for the abandonment of plot, character, even language as it had
been traditionally understood. While the Stanislavski Method
continued to dominate the Broadway stage, Brecht's epic acting
method offered the new playwrights an alternative that took
into account the presence of the actor as actor. Whereas the
Method actor was merely an instrument through which the
character created by the playwright could assume life on the
stage, the Brechtian actor remained conscious of his or her in-
dividuality while simultaneously presenting the character to the
audience.

Ionesco's hope that the theatre could rediscover "the living
image of truth" by breaking down "the false theatrical idiom"[34]
was a challenge the new American dramatists were beginning
to answer. For Ionesco, the aim of the avant-garde is to rediscover the most elementary truths about the theatre, which are
also the most easily forgotten. The place for playwrights to search
for the inner ideal of the theatre is within themselves: "for it is
in oneself that one discovers the deep and permanent foundations of theatre."[35] Alan Schneider brought Beckett's *Waiting
for Godot* to New York in 1956. This single play has probably
had the greatest impact of any individual work on the post-
modern theatre. Beckett captures the essence of theatre, ironically by moving into an area that he himself defines as alien to
the whole idea of drama:

My little exploration is the whole zone of being that has always been
set aside by artists as something unusable—as something by definition
incompatible with art.[36]

Beckett's plays attack the semblance of a rational order that conventional realistic drama presupposes. By stripping away all references other than those that can be self-generated, Beckett's plays opened the drama to an exploration of unaccommodated humanity. Ionesco acknowledged the ontological purity of Beckett's plays:

with him it is precisely the whole of the human condition which comes into play and not man in this or that society, or man seen through and distorted by a particular ideology that both simplifies and mutilates his historical and metaphysical reality, the authentic reality into which man is integrated. . . . Beckett poses the problem of the ultimate ends of man.[37]

In America, one group did more than any other to put the methods and theories of the European innovators into practice on the New York stage. Judith Malina and Julian Beck's Living Theatre endured from 1948, when it modestly began in a basement on Wooster Street, until 1964, when continual harassment by the authorities drove them into exile in Europe. But during those first seventeen years, the Living Theatre opened up enormous possibilities for the future of American drama. In 1959, their production of Jack Gelber's *The Connection* liberated the American stage by becoming the first native production of an overtly self-conscious, anti-illusionistic drama. In 1959 the importance of *The Connection* was realized by only a small group of artists and critics. In retrospect, however, we can appreciate its innovation. C.W.E. Bigsby has found that:

The Connection did potentially for American drama what Pirandello had done for Italian and indeed European drama as a whole. It dismissed a form which had ceased to serve the theatre and the purposes of drama.[38]

The historical significance of Gelber's play lies in its use of the theatre as a metaphor for the investigation of the nature of drama.

The Living Theatre was an inspiration for other theatre artists who dreamed of founding repertory companies dedicated to producing new plays and experimenting with new dramatic techniques. One of the Living Theatre's actors, Joseph Chaikin, left the company in 1963 and began his own group, the Open Theatre. A year later, Sam Shepard joined Chaikin's company. Although Shepard's direct involvement with the Open Theatre was brief, his work with them made a powerful impression on the development of his drama. And he has sustained a working relationship with Chaikin over the last twenty years. In 1979, Chaikin and Shepard wrote and produced two plays together, *Savage/Love* and *Tongues*. In 1984, they collaborated on *The War in Heaven*.

The Open Theatre extended the Living Theatre's concern with the reality of the performance as part of the world, not just a mirror of it. In *The Presence of the Actor*, Chaikin describes his purpose:

The Theatre, insofar as people are serious in it, seems to be looking for a place where it is not a duplication of life. It exists not just to make a mirror of life, but to represent a kind of realm just as certainly as music is a realm.[39]

"In former times," Chaikin believed, "acting simply meant putting on a disguise, . . . there was the old face underneath it. Now the wearing of the disguise changes the person. The stage performance informs the life performance and is informed by it."[40] The Open Theatre's interest in the transformation of the actor as a person separate from the role, through his or her experience on the stage, drew attention through reflection to the way in which a person in life creates the self by adopting various roles. "Through the working process," Chaikin declares, "the actor recreates himself."[41]

The Open Theatre's acting techniques were designed to demonstrate the freedom of the individual to escape the past and create himself or herself anew in the present by transforming fixed forms, social and psychological, that limit the possibilities for action. In her introduction to *Three Works by the Open Theatre*, Karen Malpede says that new techniques such as abandonment, receptivity, and repetition replaced the method of recall or "affective memory" derived from Stanislavski. The recall method limited the actor to his or her own repertoire of past experiences, and, more importantly, suggested that the past existed as an inexorable force determining character and action in the present.[42] The Method acting style complemented the realistic form in which an audience could anticipate a character's self to be revealed in the course of the action as physical, psychological, and social details are gradually revealed, and, particularly, as events from the past are exposed to explain action in the present.

Shepard's early plays noticeably omit such exposition scenes and thereby create the illusion that his characters have no existence prior to their appearance on the stage. Furthermore, as Bonnie Marranca points out, "the Shepard character has not simply a self but several selves which are continually changing, closer in composition to the transformational character developed by the Open Theatre than the typical dramatic character. The transformational character has a fluid relationship to changing 'realities' whereas a character in realistic drama is fixed in his relationship to reality which is itself fixed."[43]

Richard Schechner describes the transformational character in opposition to the traditional character:

In modern drama we are accustomed to the formula: actor equals character equals life. The audience sees the play and identifies with the characters and the story they enact; a "symbolic reality" is created which metaphorically recapitulates a life-experience. . . . The audience on one side and the actors on the other try to extend the character into life. . . .
Transformations introduce an entirely different kind of construction. The play is no longer a consistent set of interrelated units. . . . In transformations each scene . . . is considered separately; there is no necessary attempt to relate one scene to the next through organic development; one scene *follows* another but does not logically grow out of it. The relationship between beats, or scenes, is para-logical or pre-logical.[44]

Richard Gilman calls attention to the Open Theatre's emphasis on "transformations," exercises designed to explore the relationship between the actor's mind and the text for performance. In these improvisations, the actors were required to switch from scene to scene, character to character, without the usual psychological transitions. Gilman finds the aim of such a method unclear, but recognizes that Shepard extends these exercises by "actually writing them into his texts."[45] Gerald Weales explains Shepard's "transformations" as dramatic responses to "a feeling of a battered and broken society," and notes the wide variety in Shepard's escape/transformation endings as well as the recurrent theme of "the invention of the self," and its "transformation under pressure through release."[46] Joseph Chaikin describes one aim of the actors in the Open Theatre: "When we locate the inside of a situation in its abstract and elusive texture, we then try to make this thing *visible*."[47]

Shepard's concept of character develops from the Open Theatre's transformational exercises. He transfers the concept into his plays by allowing his characters to suddenly act out the "invisible," the inner truth of their experiences that is masked by social forms and subterfuges. Sometimes he gives the character a vaguely realistic situation in which to perform these actions—a drug-induced, hypnotic, or somnambulant state. At other times, no attempt is made to integrate these improbable transformations within any realistic convention. This method of characterization leads to some confusion for interpreters of the action, and there is a tendency to understand the actions allegorically. But Shepard's emphasis is not on equating the action of his characters with an abstraction; the emphasis is on the experience itself as a dramatic revelation of the truth of the characters' inner experiences.

Shepard's characters are actors, as Marranca indicates; like Chaikin's "real" actors, they possess a double presence—as conscious performers and as the characters they bring to life on the stage. Shepard's extension of the Open Theatre's transformation exercises becomes, in his early plays, a way of exploring the dialectical interplay between the world and the stage. Chaikin did not mean "that there is no difference between a stage performance and living . . . [but] that they are absolutely joined."[48] Shepard's dramatic career begins with an examination of this absolute fusion between the stage performance and the life performance. When they are joined, his plays are metatheatrical, a form that can lead to solipsism, self-annihilation, even nihilism in its obsessive inward turning. As his work develops, Shepard begins to experiment with forms that lead him out of the self-conscious labyrinth.

In "American Experimental Theatre: Then and Now," Shepard says:

It's become generally accepted that the other art forms are dealing with this idea [the idea of consciousness] to one degree or another. That the subject of painting is seeing. That the subject of music is hearing. That the subject of sculpture is space.[49]

But what, he asks, "is the subject of theatre which includes all of these and more?"[50] Shepard's career has been a quest for the answer to this question.

NOTES

1. John Simon, *Uneasy Stages: A Chronicle of the New York Theatre, 1963–1973* (New York: Random House, 1975), p. xiii.
2. Ibid., p. xiii.
3. Robert Brustein, *Seasons of Discontent: Dramatic Opinions, 1959–1965* (New York: Simon and Schuster, 1965), p. 14.
4. Michael Smith, introduction, *Eight Plays from Off-Off-Broadway*, eds. Nick Orzel and Michael Smith (New York: The Bobbs-Merrill Co., 1966), p. 11.
5. Ibid., p. 8.
6. Ibid., p. 5.
7. Robert J. Schroeder, ed., *The New Underground Theatre* (New York: Bantam Books, 1968), p. viii.
8. Ibid., p. vii.
9. Ibid., pp. viii-ix.
10. Ibid., p. viii.
11. Ralph Cook, "Notes on Theatre Genesis," in *Eight Plays from Off-Off-Broadway*, p. 94.
12. Ibid.
13. Schroeder, p. viii.
14. Reverend Al Carmines, "Notes on the Judson Poets' Theatre," in *Eight Plays from Off-Off-Broadway*, p. 123.
15. Ellen Stewart, "Notes on La Mama Experimental Theatre Club," in *Eight Plays from Off-Off-Broadway*, p. 164.
16. Richard Gilman, introduction, *Sam Shepard: Seven Plays* (New York: Bantam Books, 1981), p. xi.

17. Robert Brustein, *The Culture Watch: Essays on Theatre and Society, 1969–1974* (New York: Alfred A. Knopf, 1975), p. 3.

18. Ibid., p. 4.

19. Ibid., p. 38.

20. Eugène Ionesco, *Notes and Counter Notes*, trans. Donald Watson (New York: Grove Press, 1964), p. 247.

21. Ibid., p. 247.

22. Alain Robbe-Grillet, *For a New Novel: Essays on Fiction*, trans. Richard Howard (New York: Grove Press, 1965), pp. 157–158.

23. Brustein, *Seasons of Discontent*, p. 276.

24. Ibid., p. 280.

25. Richard Gilman, "The Drama is Coming Now," in *The Modern American Theatre: A Collection of Critical Essays*, ed. Alvin B. Kernan (Englewood Cliffs, N.J.: Prentice-Hall, Inc., 1967), p. 159.

26. Ibid. Gilman believes further that "all the representative art of our time is marked by a questioning—implicit or otherwise, . . . of the very nature, purpose, and validity of art itself." Pointing out the pervasiveness of this questioning, he mentions Picasso, Stravinsky, Joyce , Kafka, Pirandello, Brecht, Mann, the surrealists, Jackson Pollock, Beckett, Antonioni, Ionesco, Nabokov, and Genet.

27. Lionel Abel, *Metatheatre: A New View of Dramatic Form* (New York: Hill and Wang, 1963).

28. June Schlueter, *Metafictional Characters in Modern Drama* (New York: Columbia University Press, 1979).

29. Sam Shepard, "Metaphors, Mad Dogs, and Old Time Cowboys," an interview with Kenneth Chubb et al., *Theatre Quarterly*, 4, No. 15 (1974), p. 5.

30. Ibid.

31. Gilman, introduction, p. xi.

32. Michael Smith, "Theatre: *Cowboys* and *The Rock Garden*," *The Village Voice*, 22 October 1964, p. 13.

33. Simon, *Uneasy Stages*, p. 13.

34. Ionesco, p. 33.

35. Ibid., p. 48.

36. Samuel Beckett, an interview with Israel Shenker, *New York Times*, 6 May 1956, sec. 2, p. 3.

37. Ionesco, p. 135.

38. C. W. E. Bigsby, *Confrontation and Commitment: A Study of Contemporary American Drama, 1959–1966* (London: MacGibbon and Kee, 1967), p. 10.

39. Joseph Chaikin, *The Presence of the Actor* (New York: Atheneum, 1972), p. 25.

40. Ibid., p. 6.

41. Ibid.

42. Karen Malpede, introduction, *Three Works by the Open Theatre* (New York: Drama Book Specialists, 1974), p. 15.

43. Bonnie Marranca, "Alphabetical Shepard: The Play of Words," in *American Dreams: The Imagination of Sam Shepard*, ed. Bonnie Marranca (New York: The Performing Arts Journal Press, 1981), p. 14.

44. Richard Schechner, introduction, *Viet Rock and Other Plays*, by Megan Terry (New York: Simon and Schuster, 1967), p. 13–14.

45. Gilman, introduction, p. xv.

46. Gerald Weales, "The Transformations of Sam Shepard," in *American Dreams*, p. 38.

47. Joseph Chaikin, "The Open Theatre," *TDR* 9, No. 2, p. 193.

48. Chaikin, *Presence of the Actor*, p. 6.

49. Sam Shepard, "American Experimental Theatre: Then and Now," *Performing Arts Journal*, 2, No. 2 (Fall 1977), p. 13.

50. Ibid.

III

"THE PLAY'S THE THING":
METAPHORICAL STAGES

They were explosions that were coming out of some kind of inner turmoil in me that I didn't understand at all. . . . They were just survival techniques, a means of putting something outside rather than having it all inside.[1]

Shepard refers to his early plays as "survival kits" that he began writing with "the hope of extending the sensation of 'play' (as in 'kid') on into adult life."[2] And, indeed, one of the earliest responses to Shepard's work by an English critic was " 'Childlike': . . . whatever else Mr. Shepard be, he is certainly not loaded down: he writes plays literally like a child, cantilevering his fantasies out over void in complete confidence that sooner or later they will reach solid ground on the other side."[3] Shepard's first play, _Cowboys_ (1964), is now lost (Patti Smith, the rock singer who lived with Shepard for a brief period in the Chelsea Hotel, says that Shepard wrote his first play "in true pioneer style" and, in keeping with the childlike persona—on the back of used Tootsie Roll wrappers).[4]

COWBOYS #2

In 1967 Shepard wrote _Cowboys #2_, a close rewrite of the lost original _Cowboys_, which is treated here conceptually as Shepard's first play. In certain respects, _Cowboys #2_ is derivative of Beckett, whom Shepard acknowledges as an influence. The play that opened up the unlimited potential of words for Shepard was _Waiting for Godot_. Although he disclaims its formal effect, it did make him suddenly aware "that with words you could do *anything*."[5]

In Shepard's first one-act play, a sawhorse affixed with a blinking yellow caution light stands singularly in the center of a bare stage, recalling the isolated tree of *Waiting for Godot*. Shepard's prop, however, appropriately locates his two main characters, urban cowboys dressed in identical black pants, shirts, vests, and hats. Seated on either side of the sawhorse, Chet and Stu appear to be television adaptations of American mythic heroes, stranded in an urban world where only the sound of a single cricket's chirp serves as a reminder of their past. The characters' lack of motive, purpose, or direction indicates Shepard's debt to the absurdist tradition.

Chet and Stu begin their dialogue with a cue from the offstage voice of Man #1: "It's going to rain."[6] Without acknowledging the offstage speaker, the cowboys begin to discuss the weather, the possibility of rain, and the effect of a downpour on their clothes, which are much in need of laundering. Rather than developing this superficial dialogue into revealing interaction that would lend psychological substance to his characters, Shepard elects to emphasize the theatricality of their action when Chet crosses downstage to observe some cloud formations and adopts the attitude, stance, gestures, and speech patterns of an oldtime cowboy. Stu responds to Chet's improvisation by accepting his new name, Mel, and his new role as Chet's old crony (whom he now calls Clem). Before an audience can even begin to localize or identify these characters, they enter an imaginary landscape and become someone else. The roles they adopt have no identifiable purpose; they are not, for example, in disguise—they are simply "playing."

After a brief discussion about the weather, Stu summons Chet back upstage and out of the improvisation by calling to him in his normal voice and by his real name. Stu then takes a turn initiating the game, and Chet follows his cues until Stu exhausts his creative potential in the role by faltering in his search for a simile to describe the cloud formations. Chet becomes impatient with his friend's interruption of their game; Stu becomes angry as he fumbles for words, disturbing the smooth flow of their play. But the imaginary rain cools their tempers, and the game resumes as Stu and Chet (now Mel and Clem again) imagine they are cowboys in Red Valley.

In the recesses between their improvisations, their dialogue reveals very little about their characters. Their vapid conversations seem to be ways of filling the time until their next sequence of games. Chet and Stu's dialogue strongly resembles Estragon and Vladimir's in its comic repetitions and aimlessness. For example, Stu suddenly begins doing jumping calisthenics and the conversation follows:

Stu: Clap, clap, clap. Clapping, clapping. Clap.

Chet: What are you doing?

Stu: This?

Chet: That.

Stu: Oh. Well, you remember yesterday?

Chet: Yesterday what?

Stu: Remember yesterday when I was sitting and my feet fell asleep?

Chet: Yeah.

Stu: Well, this is for that. (p. 135)

When they enter the world of their imaginary play, however, Stu and Chet perform with liveliness and utter conviction. In the next segment of their game, Stu and Chet pretend to hold off an Indian attack, while the sound effects of horses charging, guns firing, and Indians screaming accompany their improvisation. When Stu pretends to be wounded, Chet breaks off the imaginary arrow from his friend's arm and crosses downstage to scoop up a hatful of water for the injured cowboy.

The fourth wall convention is violated when Chet reaches across the edge of the stage as if it were the bank of a stream. Up until this moment in the play, the distinction between Chet and Stu, the characters, and Clem and Mel, the characters impersonated, has remained apparent. But when Chet throws the fanciful water from the bankside in Stu's face, Stu responds to the action in his own character rather than as the oldtimer he has been playing. Stu becomes furious with Chet for dousing him with the water, and Chet does not consider offering the obvious excuse that the water is not real and that they are only playing a game. Instead, he offers vain apologies while Stu withdraws into private reveries. In Shepard's play, the improvisation simply, and quite inexplicably, becomes real for the role-playing characters. The influence of the Open Theatre's transformational exercises is evident here as the actors' warm-ups become part of Shepard's concept of character. This theatrical model of character as actor is typical of the early plays. It was not until the early seventies that Shepard began to think seriously of other models for character construction. In the early plays, the conventional concept of character as an integrated whole held little appeal for him. Instead he preferred "a character that was constantly unidentifiable, shifting through the actor, so that the actor could play anything, and the audience was never expected to identify with the character."[7] When Peter Brook asked him the simple question, "What is character?" Shepard began to seriously question the "mystery" and "simplicity" of the concept.[8]

Shepard also used language unconventionally, as the next scene demonstrates, when Stu, oblivious to Chet's entreaties, launches into long monologues laden with images of death and decay. Lamenting man's corruption of nature, Stu speaks of "peacock feathers left in vases until the stems rot and the water gets all smelly and green . . . dead turtles with painted shells left to rot in slimy water . . . chickens penned up whose feet rot after a while from walking in their own crap"(p. 147). During Stu's monologue the sound of car horns offstage grows increasingly louder, overpowering the sound of crickets chirping that we have heard since the beginning of the play. As Stu's grotesque imagery bemoans a natural world degraded by man, the offstage sound effects suggest an urban world impinging upon the ideal landscape of the old West. Here Shepard does allow his character some oblique social commentary, but Stu's monologue does not have the direct effect of castigating America's crude materialism, nor is it primarily revelatory of Stu's psychology. Like many of the surrealists, Shepard's language is not designed to communicate social or psychological concepts; rather, its effect is emotional, hypnotic, imagistic. Shepard himself uses the word "incantatory," although he disdains association with surrealism:

the power of words for me isn't so much in the delineation of a character's social circumstances as it is in the capacity to evoke visions in the eye of the audience. *Words as living incantations and not as symbols.*[9] (emphasis mine)

Like Artaud, Shepard is drawn to primitive cultures and the heroic past where ritualistic and instinctual life have precedence over civilization's cognitive structures. Both writers prefer the pre-logical or para-logical to the logical. Shepard's own comments on his radical use of language echo Artaud's:

To make metaphysics out of a spoken language is to make the language express what it does not ordinarily express; to make use of it in a new, exceptional, and unaccustomed fashion; to reveal its possibilities for producing physical shock . . . to turn against language and its basely utilitarian, one could say, alimentary sources . . . and finally *to consider language as the form of Incantation.*[10] (emphasis mine)

As the real world threatens to overcome the private play of the characters, Stu is jolted out of his daydream by Chet's catalogue of the pleasures of eating and the simultaneous offstage voices of Man #1 and Man #2 discussing the price of food and rent. The discussion of everyday realities reawakens Chet and Stu's fantasies and they escape again into their roles. Ross Wetzsteon points out that Shepard's monologues are not obscure "unrealistic leaps of imagination," but "purely naturalistic" in their direct revelation of the reality of his characters' consciousness: "Shepard realizes that fantasies constitute a great deal of our conscious life, and that they are thus as real as, and often more revealing than, our behavior."[11]

In the final scene of his first play, Shepard combines character, language, and action to blur the distinction between theatre and life, reinforcing his emphasis on the metaphorical reality of the world as stage. As Chet urges Stu to help him search for shade to protect them from the devastating rays of the sun, the technical effects once again reinforce the characters' game as the lights grow brighter until by the end of the play they

have reached full brightness. Chet then enters his role with
dire seriousness, but Stu falls asleep and fails to respond to his
partner's feverish efforts to find the shade. Chet is now playing
the game to survive; but Stu is not playing at all. Chet, in fact,
no longer considers their improvisation to be diverting or
amusing. He screams at Stu: "Okay, Stu, this isn't funny. I
don't think this is funny. You're going to sleep all day while I
bust my ass looking for shade?" (p. 151). Chet then imagines
that vultures are circling overhead and he frantically addresses
the birds: "This ain't no joke you shitty birds! What do you
think this is? T.V. or something?" (p. 152), a comic assertion of
the dire effects that result from a confusion of "play" and reality.

Chet drags the sleeping Stu up and down the stage looking
for shade and continues to insist upon the reality of the characters' play as Man #1 and Man #2 finally appear onstage. The
two unnamed characters are the same age as Chet and Stu but
are dressed in suits. As they walk onstage, they begin reading
from the scripts in their hands—copies of *Cowboys #2*. The play
ends with all four characters onstage, Stu and Chet upstage as
the latter tries to ward off the vultures and protect his friend
from the scorching heat, while downstage Man #1 and Man
#2 read in a monotone. As the sound of car horns, screaming
Indians, and galloping horses builds in volume and blends to
the end of the play, we may well exclaim with Pirandello's
manager, "Pretence? Reality? To hell with it all!" [12]

In *Cowboys #2* Shepard essentially is experimenting with the
possibilities of the stage and the implications of performance.
Man #1 and Man #2 are characters who impersonate actors,
either very bad ones or actors engaged in an initial read-through
of a script. Thus we are reminded, in case we have become lost
in the illusion, that *Cowboys #2* is merely a play and that Chet
and Stu are simply players. Chet and Stu are, of course, actors
impersonating characters who are engaged in creative role-
playing. Shepard's characters, however, differ from the conventional dramatic character since they have little or no identity outside their onstage improvisation. They exist primarily in
the play within the play; their role-playing becomes for them a
reality. Their behavior is different from the actions of a dra-

matic character who becomes what he is pretending to be as a function of circumstances within the fictive reality of the play. Hamlet, for example, adopts his antic disposition as a subterfuge, a mask to disarm and deceive other characters in the play, and then, arguably, he becomes mad indeed. Pirandello's Henry IV is the classic example of a modern character whose role becomes reality, but in Pirandello's play we are at least given a realistic situation as an initial premise in the play (Henry IV's fall from his horse and subsequent belief that he is the character that he was impersonating in the pageant). But like Henry IV at the end of Pirandello's play, Shepard's characters become prisoners of their own game, incapable of existing outside their self-created artifice.

In *Cowboys #2* there is only a minimal suggestion of a world outside the stage action. If it were not for the age of the actors who play Chet and Stu, it would be nearly impossible to differentiate between the characters as young men and the old-timers they impersonate. Shepard does indeed extend the idea of child's play into the mature characters' action in this first one-act play. Kenneth Chubb, the artistic director of England's Wakefield Tricycle Company, has recorded some of the difficulties he encountered directing this play. Since Shepard offers no real information about his characters, an actor "faces the problem of bringing his own personality to the character without the support of the conventional ways of acting and reacting that most actors use convincingly to present a character."[13]

Shepard's unconventional characters are at home in his dramatic structures, which also counter tradition. Through directing Shepard, Chubb found that:

Instead of actions, characters, situations and dialogue all working together to present a plot or central idea, Sam's plays are mosaics of different colours and textures that present an abstract rather than a formal pattern. We have come to accept this basic theory in music and painting but not in the theatre.[14]

The meager narrative in *Cowboys #2* does not refer an audience to a world outside the stage action. By presenting the performance as an ultimate reality without reference to an action in the world that is imitated, Shepard's play insists upon a metaphorical reality common to the world and the stage, and calls attention to its own artifice. *Cowboys #2* takes imitation as its subject and is thus an example of almost pure metatheatre.

As Shepard's dramaturgy develops, he begins to flesh out the skeletal structure of his first play and his idea of character gradually assumes a more conventional form. Shepard describes his characters as "unknown quantities": he begins with images, some visual, some auditory. He sees, for example, "an old man by a broken car in the middle of nowhere and those simple elements right away set up associations and yearnings to pursue what he is doing there."[15] Like Pirandello's six characters who appear before the author in his study, Shepard's characters "appear out of nowhere in three dimensions and speak," but not directly to him because he is "not in the play," but "watching it."[16] Shepard sees his role as a playwright as essentially that of a spectator or an actor. The playwright, he says, "is the only character who gets to play all the parts."[17]

CHICAGO

In *Chicago* (1966) Shepard's main character creates and directs the action of the play from the center of a bare stage where he sits splashing water in a bathtub. Stu's opening monologue suggests the prattle of a child who is enjoying the sound of his own voice and reveling in the discovery of nonsensical rhyme:

> "So ya say. What a day.
> In the hay. Anyway.
> And ya walk through the town
> and around."[18]

Stu continues to chatter as his girlfriend, Joy, calls out to him that the biscuits are ready. Instead of responding to her call by leaving the bathtub and going into the offstage kitchen for breakfast, Stu seizes upon "biscuits" as a cue for more inane babbling. His failure to reply within the framework of recognizably realistic action thwarts the audience's anticipation of a readily accessible conflict. Stu may be suffering from some mental defect or psychological disturbance, but Shepard does not develop this possibility. It seems, instead, that Stu is simply engaged in creative play-making. Shepard's "Notes to the Actors" in his preface to *Angel City* could equally serve as clues to the concept underlying Stu's character in *Chicago*:

Instead of the idea of a "whole character" with logical motives behind his behavior which the actor submerges himself into, he should consider instead a fractured whole with bits and pieces of character flying off the central theme. In other words, more in terms of collage construction or jazz improvisation.[19]

For a moment it appears that Stu will leave his bathtub and join Joy in the kitchen; instead, he sits back down with a towel over his head and begins to imitate an old woman chastising young girls for "paradin' around in (their) flimsies" (p. 5).

Once involved in this new game, Stu stays in character to respond to Joy's anger about the cold biscuits. When we hear Joy's voice offstage answering a telephone call, a reason is suggested for Stu's withdrawal into child's play and role-playing. Joy, we learn, has accepted a job in another city and is preparing to leave. Stu clearly has difficulty accepting the imminent separation and adopts a mask to conceal his fear and hostility. Joy also practices evasion as can be seen in the following dialogue which is Pinteresque in its surface simplicity and subtextual complexity:

Stu: Did you say you got the job? Did I hear you say that?

Joy: I said Myra's coming.

Stu: On the phone. Did you say you got the job?

Joy: Yes. (Stu stands suddenly in the tub and starts yelling.)

Stu: You did not!

Joy: Yes!

Stu: They hired you!

Joy: Yes!

Stu: Good! I'm really glad!

Joy: Good!

Stu: I'm really, really glad. When are you going?

Joy: Oh, I don't know.

Stu: You don't?

Joy: Soon.

Stu: Good. (p. 7)

Joy then comes onstage and initiates the game that they are out in the water alone on a boat when she climbs into the bathtub with Stu. Stu protests but resumes his disguise as an old woman and within the safety of this innocuous role frees himself to vent some of the hostility he feels toward Joy. As Joy dangles her arm over the side of the "boat" encouraging Stu to play with her, he tells her that the water is full of starving barracudas, just ready to devour a nice young virgin like her. He even tries to push her overboard into the hungry jaws of the fish. Deeply committed to the game, Joy grapples with Stu in genuine terror.

As long as Joy remains offstage her language and action are mundanely realistic. But onstage she enters the fantasy world of Stu's imagination. When her friends begin to arrive, the onstage and offstage worlds collide. Her four companions appear one by one carrying suitcases for the impending journey as well as fishing poles. These props signal the crossing over of Stu's fantasy world into the "real life" action of Joy and her friends. Just as the improvisation of Chet and Stu in *Cowboys #2* becomes interwoven with and finally inseparable from the reality of the characters, so in *Chicago* Stu's imaginary world breaks through the confined environment of the bathtub (which is clearly an objectification of his consciousness) and crosses over into the story of Joy and her departure. The fourth wall becomes a bankside again, as it was in *Cowboys #2*, as the four friends cast their fishing lines over the end of the stage. Stu finally leaves his bathtub, walks to the edge of the stage, and directly addresses the audience. Like a swimming instructor preparing his class before they venture into the water, Stu coaches the audience to breathe in unison with him.

Isolated in the bathtub, Stu had been unable to join the world outside his imagination. His fantasies take shape in images and fragmented narratives that function as objective correlatives for his repressed emotions. Stu escapes into play where he is free to express his anger, resentment, and fear without the repercussions that the cramping environment of the external world might afford. The game becomes a compensatory device, a vicarious method of satisfying an unfulfilled wish. This form of play closely resembles the shape of a dream, and thus Stu's monologues are like the "unfettered fancies, absurdities, and improvisations" of Strindberg's *A Dream Play*.[20] As Stu's private fantasies come to dominate the shape and action of the play, the other characters become less and less realistic. By the end of the play Joy is crossing the stage mechanically from left to right with her suitcases in a red wagon; her four friends are sitting numbly on the edge of the stage casting their fishing lines—they have become the "hung up" fishermen of Stu's fancy.

Ralph Cook's director's notes to *Chicago* clearly indicate the metatheatrical context of the play and the self-consciousness of the protagonist:

The only continuously real elements were Stu, a bathtub, a towel, and soap. The other actors, offstage rooms, and props were forces working upon his reality . . . the bathtub exists *on a stage in front of an audience*. The set is black and as perfectly symmetrical and simple as possible. The offstage party sounds are heard only when Stu hears them.[21] (emphasis mine)

In essence, Shepard's play is then a monologue describing the artist's consciousness as represented by the main character who defines reality in a solipsistic exercise. Cook's notes indicate that even the fragile objective world that appears through the manifestations of Stu's fantasies is "utterly destroyed when the guests become fishermen."[22] Through denial and repression, Stu successfully subsumes the objective world into his own subjective vision. The performance operates as a metaphor for the consciousness of the playwright-as-Stu, the only actor who can play all the parts, creator, performer, and director. The mixture of realism and fantasy and the logic of a dream provide a structure for the exploration of Stu's controlling consciousness. Stu becomes a master playmaker who dictates action and defines the reality of the world as a product of his own imagination.

LA TURISTA

In the plays that followed *Chicago*, Shepard began to create a more concrete world that defines, and confines, the consciousness of his characters. His sets become more formidable spaces for the characters to transcend as his stages begin to represent recognizable social worlds. In his first full-length play, *La Turista* (1967), Kent and Salem, American tourists in Mexico, sit stiffly propped on twin beds in their motel room, severely sunburned and suffering from dysentery, the "la turista" of the title. The stage-as-stage is transformed into a local habitation in Shepard's indictment of American society. As their cigarette brand names testify, Kent and Salem are products of unhealthy American society. While they browse through *Time* and *Life*, the couple rest comfortably, smug and self-satisfied, discussing their maladies, secure in their pseudo-physiological analysis. Kent explains to Salem that sunburn is caused by the "molecular destruction of the fatty tissue by the sun's rays," reassuring her that there is nothing magical or inexplicable about their red skin, "just the blood rushing to the surface to repair the damage."[23]

Impressed with his own analysis, Kent contemplates anthropological theories on the origin of dark-skinned races, concluding that skin color is nature's camouflage, a way of "deceiving death" (p. 258). Salem also poses as a medical expert when she describes the symptoms of diarrhea, satisfied that her high metabolism will protect her from the disease that afflicts Kent. Both tourists take refuge in their composed analysis which insulates them from fear and uncertainty. The couple's rhetorical poses generate an illusion of certainty that quickly surrenders to fantasy when Kent bursts into a visionary aria on the nature of third-degree burns:

"You become a flame and dance in mid-air. The bottom is blue. The middle is yellow and changes to green. The top is red and changes to orange. The breeze dances with you. The flame reaches up and then shrinks and bursts into sparks. The ground bursts into flame and circles the breeze. The sparks dart through the breeze and dash back and forth hitting up against the flames, and. . . . " (p. 260)

Kent's fantastic verbal transmutation is interrupted by the sudden intrusion of a Mexican boy who sends him scurrying under the bedsheets for cover. Despite the couple's offer of money from their overstuffed suitcases, an image of excessive American materialism, the intractable boy refuses to leave, rips the telephone out of the wall, and spits in Kent's face, sending him screaming into the bathroom where he is overcome by another wave of dysentery.

In the struggle between the American tourists and the Mexican boy, Shepard demonstrates his view of America, a sterile, isolated country, out of touch with everyday realities encountered by other cultures, perilously pure, uncontaminated. The central image in the play is sterility, with all of its ambiguous connotations, reinforced by the medicinal language of the tourists, and powerfully rendered in Kent's monologue in the image of his body fusing with the natural elements in a flame that burns in isolation consuming itself. The Mexican boy, who Kent imagines sleeps on the dirt and sells dirty Coca-Cola bottles to passing tourists, defiles the tourists' sterile shelter, his threatening presence attested to by the comically exaggerated reactions of fear and revulsion by Kent and Salem. The intrusion of the Mexican boy reveals the tourists' shallow defenses, but the real threat is exposed when Kent emerges from the bathroom transformed into a cowboy wearing a Panamanian hat, a linen shirt, handmade boots, and a pistol around his waist. He struts across the stage hitching his pistol on his hip, a "new man," the rugged frontier individual with a built-in immunity to his environment and a changed attitude toward his homeland. Disguised as the quintessential American hero of the mythic West, Kent declares modern America his enemy, "an isolated land of purification" that breeds people who are so unresistant to any foreign elements that soon they will be unable to travel outside the country, and "foreigners won't be able to come in [because] they won't be able to take the cleanliness" (p. 267). Kent's monologue ends in a warning vision: " Extinction! Destruction! Rot and Ruin! I see it all now clearly before me! The Greatest Society on its way Downhill!" (p. 268). The cowboy persona frees Kent to criticize the hidden evils of modern American society; but Shepard also emphasizes the vulnerability of our nation's mythic hero in this scene. Kent's cowboy costume is lacking in one article—his pants. As he struts around in his underwear, his appearance comically undercuts his patronizing rhetoric. His performance comes to an abrupt halt when he faints upon discovering the Mexican boy in bed with Salem. Thus American mythical history and modern American society are equally impotent and disempowered.

Through rhetorical posturing and role-playing, Shepard's characters attempt to escape from the horrifying reality of their present existence, in which they are shown to be products of a barren, sterile culture. The fantastic transformations are woven into an essentially naturalistic fabric with no attempt to integrate the two forms.

The characters that we meet in the beginning of the play are plastic cultural images hiding behind mindlessly adopted masks. They have come to Mexico to escape; as Kent says, he came here "to disappear for awhile" (p. 259). When Elizabeth Hardwick saw the play at the American Place Theatre, the audience in attendance apparently had much in common with Shepard's depiction of stereotypical middle-class Americans. She described the spectators as, "for the most part, utterly depressing; middle-aged, middle-class, and rather aggressively indifferent: a dead weight of alligators, dozing and grunting before muddily sliding away."[24] If that audience had come to the theatre to escape from themselves for a while, they would have been as sorely disappointed with Shepard's play as his characters were disillusioned with their vacation in Mexico.

As the play progresses, the pseudo-self that is Kent's superficial mask disappears as he is transformed. The first transformation takes shape as a sudden linguistic expansion when Kent's dry, analytical prose explodes into the visionary, poetic aria in which he imagines himself a flame fusing with the natural elements on the burning desert. This shift in rhetoric signals the existence of an aspect of his character previously concealed.

In a similar scene, Kent's matter-of-fact, rational analysis of his sunburn suddenly enlarges to include a fanciful description of "fourth degree burns." Ibsen's brilliant parody of the romantic apotheosis of self in the onion-peeling scene in *Peer Gynt* comes to mind when Kent and Salem argue about the number of layers of skin that can be peeled away from their scorched bodies. Kent's second linguistic flight is occasioned by his insistence that there is a fourth layer of skin yet to be discovered and named. "There's only three layers you know," Salem tells him; "it doesn't go on forever" (p. 259). Refusing to accept this obvious fact, Kent insists: "Obviously you've never heard of the fourth degree burn. A fourth degree burn is unheard of because it's never happened, but one day it will, and doctors will be dismayed from coast to coast, and a new word will be born into their language" (p. 259). When the last layer of Ibsen's onion is stripped away in *Peer Gynt*, the revelation that there is nothing at the center is, of course, meant to strip away the hero's illusions. But Shepard's hero believes in his dreams of another layer of skin yet to be discovered, just as he believes in the ability to create a self out of nothing.

But Kent's rhapsodies fail to conjure his dreams into existence, and as the sordid reality of the Mexican boy's presence in bed with Salem impinges upon Kent's consciousness, he faints. Kent's response to the confrontation with the Mexican boy who usurps his place in Salem's bed suggests his own impotence, or, at the least, his disempowerment. Thus Shepard strikes another chord in the multiple implications of the sterility theme. Significantly, also, the boy refers to Salem as "Mom," and, as Ron Mottram points out, the oedipal overtones in this triangular relationship anticipate Shepard's lengthy exploration of family psychology in the later plays.[25] When a witchdoctor and his apprentice son arrive to cure Kent, the young Mexican boy remains to explain the ritual and its purpose to the audience who are now asked to assume the role of tourists. The boy poses as a knowledgeable guide who skillfully describes the ritual, demystifying it for the "tourists" by explaining it in terms of an ancient rite performed for the benefit of people in the village who "are very superstitious and still believe in spirits possessing the body" (p. 271). This scene recalls Kent and

Salem's former conviction that there is nothing mysterious or magical about their condition, and comments ironically on Kent who now appears to be possessed.

As the witchdoctor performs the ritual, another transformation occurs when the Mexican boy dresses in Kent's clothing, which has been removed by the witchdoctor's son. As he assumes Kent's "mask" he also begins to play Kent's role as Salem's comforter. In a final effort to remove the intractable boy from the motel room, Salem leads him into the audience who assume the role of villagers in the marketplace. But when the boy returns to the stage, responding to a telephone call summoning him home, Salem suddenly changes her mind and begins pleading with him to stay, offering him material rewards and transport to America. Act I comes to an irresolute end as Salem begs the Mexican boy to remain with her and Kent lies inertly on the floor, the spirit within unexorcised by the repetitive, uninspired ritual performed by the witchdoctor.

The sickness that Kent and Salem suffer cannot be cured by the primitive rituals of the past, and the sterile forms of the present have been invaded and shown to lack strength and resilience. The tourists' cozy refuge has been ravaged, just as their bodies have been devastated by the foreign amoeba. "You're both dead" (p. 274) the Mexican boy tells Salem as she protests ineffectually. Act II does not bring Salem and Kent back to life, for in it they enact a parallel scenario as the scene shifts to the past action that led to Kent and Salem's escape to Mexico. In an American hotel, a doctor in Civil War uniform ministers to Kent with results as futile as those of the witchdoctor. The past, represented by the two doctors, cannot recover the self, reveal inner truth, or give meaning to the present for these contemporary characters. Their only route to authenticity is through a determined act of recreation.

In the second act, Kent begins to "disappear" as he announced he would do in Act I. Salem describes his disease to the doctor: "We'll be talking back and forth and we'll be not necessarily deeply involved in what we're saying, but nevertheless talking. And he'll gradually begin to go away" (p. 281). When the doctor fails to understand, Salem explains that a person can simply "disappear . . . while we're talking" (p. 281).

At a loss without symptoms, runny nose, aching back, "things that show on the outside what the inside might be up to" (p. 282), the doctor finally diagnoses "sleeping sickness" to explain Kent's recurrent pattern of walking, talking, yawning, and sleeping. Here Shepard mocks the American whose consciousness is lowered in ignorance and apathy to a state that is scarcely above the level of automatism. Shepard demonstrates one of his strongest talents as a dramatist by presenting this malady directly rather than having it discussed in the dialogue. As Ross Wetzsteon points out, "It is [Shepard's] genius to provide us not with the symptoms but with the disease, not with the outside but with the inside."[26] The doctor's language in this scene echoes Kent's self-analysis in Act I, again parodying the rhetoric of science and medicine that is used to disguise the doctor's inability to understand Kent's malady.

For the remainder of the play, Kent remains in a somnambulant state, as the stage directions tell us, existing in "a world unrelated to anything on stage" (p. 284). While Kent is trapped in his private world, the other characters become prisoners in the hotel room. The telephone is disconnected, thwarting Salem's efforts to make airplane reservations to Mexico where the couple can escape. Each character's objective becomes an attempt to make an exit. Kent holds an imaginary gun on the doctor, accusing him of plotting to perform an experiment on a "dying man." The doctor pulls a real pistol on Kent and accuses him in turn of putting ideas into his head and forcing him to "transform the dying man into a thing of beauty" (p. 294). In an elaborate allusion to *Frankenstein* (more derivative of movie adaptations than true to the original), Kent imagines himself transformed into the monster with the doctor/creator in pursuit. He describes himself rising from the stainless steel table, bursting the leather bonds, and escaping as he leaps off the stage into the auditorium. Kent's final action calls attention once again to the metatheatrical nature of Shepard's early plays. He rejects the role imposed upon him by the doctor, insists upon controlling his own transformation, and when he is forced back onto the stage to resume his role, he leaps through the upstage wall leaving the cut-out silhouette of his figure as the play's final image.

Kent's flight into the auditorium and his final escape through the upstage wall fulfills the escape/transformation pattern described by Gerald Weales. His action does reflect Shepard's "response to a battered and broken society."[27] The prevalent theme of the individual in conflict with society in the American drama of the decade is depicted by Shepard through Kent's unique hallucinatory vision. Arthur Ganz finds the themes of escape and transcendence that have dominated modern drama since its inception beckoning still in this strikingly modern play in which Kent's concluding leap "suggests [that] the realm on the further side of reality and the desire to attain it are still part of our dramatic imagination."[28]

Difficulties in responding to La Turista no doubt arise from Shepard's lack of concentrated shaping of its many parts into a unified whole. Although Act II was revised for production under the direction of Jacques Levy, most of the play was written "in a semidelirious state of severe dysentery." Suffering from "la turista" himself "almost anything [he] could manage to write seemed valid."[29] Nevertheless, the bizarrely unfocused vision of the twenty-three-year-old playwright captures the frenzied, fragmented existence of contemporary life. Elizabeth Hardwick, who reviewed the first production, found a satisfying unity in La Turista, despite its apparent formlessness:

You do not feel you are being given a package, assembled for a purpose, and in some way this is disconcerting to the senses. The audience, accustomed to ensembles created as a calculation, may feel left out. . . . [But] in the long run, what is so beautiful is the graceful—in spite of the frenzied energy—concentration of the work as a whole.[30]

In the broader tradition, Shepard shares the distinctive traits of the "greatest American authors"—Hawthorne, Melville, Twain, and James among them—who Richard Poirier finds "try against the perpetually greater power of reality, to create an environment that might allow some longer existence to the hero's momentary expansion of consciousness."[31] In Kent's final monumental monologue we can see affinities with the American hero whose "imagination of the self . . . has no economic, or social, or sexual objectification." Kent substitutes himself for the world, and in his private domain there exists "a world elsewhere."[32]

Although Shepard's play is critical of society, it is not a simple indictment of America. It would be reductive to suggest that Shepard's play rests firmly in the genre of social criticism. The playwright's insistence that he is not interested in social issues at all may sound disingenuous given the rather direct criticism of society in *La Turista*; nevertheless, the play is not principally a diatribe on American materialism and isolationism and certainly the play does not yield any clear or overt social criticism.[33] Kent's action is more a response to his metaphysical dilemma, his lack of identity, than to the external world. *La Turista* answers Artaud's call for a theatre that does not seek "to resolve social and psychological conflicts, but to express objectively certain secret truths that have been buried under forms in their encounter with Becoming."[34] Kent's erratic efforts to escape, through flight or transformation, are all responses to his fear of confrontation with the reality of his situation. On the one hand, Kent says that he wants to disappear, to lose himself; on the other hand, he tries out various roles in an effort to "find himself." He rejects any solution that is not of his own making, in particular, the doctor's offer to perform a lobotomy that would make him one with nature, "peeling the scalp away neatly. Carving out the stickiness and placing cool summer breezes inside" (p. 294). The union with nature could offer Kent a momentary release from the burden of self-consciousness, as it does for O'Neill's Edmund in *Long Day's Journey Into Night* for example, who discovered a transient freedom as he "dissolved in the sea, became white sails and flying spray, became beauty and rhythm."[35] Shepard's character rejects this possible freedom.

La Turista offers no final solution to the metaphysical questions it engenders and it provides no resolution for Kent and Salem, for although Kent's final leap suggests that he has at last seized control of his own action, Shepard's transposition of the temporal sequence of the play (Act II occurring first in time) intimates that Kent "escapes" into Act I, on vacation in Mexico, bearing with him all of his country's ills in an inescapable pattern from which there is no exit. But the play fulfills the demand voiced by O'Neill, the first American playwright to boldly experiment with dramatic themes that centered on the question of individual response to reality:

The playwright of today must dig at the roots of the sickness of today as he feels it—the death of the Old God and the failure of science and materialism to give any satisfying new one for the surviving primitive religious instinct to find a meaning of life in and to comfort his fear of death in.[36]

THE TOOTH OF CRIME

In *The Tooth of Crime* (1972) Shepard broadens the basis of his hero's quest by posing a metaphysical conflict in a classical mythic form. The plot of the play begins near the end of the hero's story, at a critical juncture in the hero's quest for his true nature. As Ruby Cohn points out, "like classical tragedy, *The Tooth of Crime* begins close to its climax: Hoss needs a kill."[37] The dramatic action culminates in a classical agon, a sacred combat between the Old King and the new. Hoss, the aging rock star, struggles to understand, control, and maintain the image of himself dictated by the past, which is disintegrating under self-scrutiny. Crow, a gypsy usurper, marks Hoss for destruction and plans to expose Hoss's image as a projected fantasy which he will replace with his own reality. As the play begins, Hoss has arrived at a critical moment in his search for self-identification. As in classical tragedy, the early scenes are devoted to Hoss's suffering and confusion as he prepares for an inevitable destiny that will be determined in the outcome of a climactic duel of words with Crow, the lone individual who will assume Hoss's power and position after completing his *rite de passage.*

At the same time that Shepard manipulates and modernizes the ancient myth, he exposes and attempts to deconstruct a purely theatrical world, represented in the play by the rock music industry, by revealing and stripping away the illusions of a hero whose self-concept is singular and idealistic. Hoss's opening song, "The Way Things Are," introduces a conflict between a world of appearances and his private concept of reality that remains a fundamental reference of the play. Alone on stage, Hoss rises from his throne and performs a solo for the audience that begins:

> "So here's another illusion to add to your confusion
> Of the way things are . . .
> So here's another fantasy
> About the way things seem to be to me . . ."[38]

Thus Shepard immediately establishes that his hero's perceptions of reality are fantastic and illusory. Hoss's self-conscious recognition of his own subjective vision implies some internal conflict, and alerts the audience to search for a reality that supplants the hero's illusion. Therefore, deciphering ambiguous language becomes the spectator's initial task. In the opening dialogue Hoss speaks of his next "hit" and desire to secure a gold record, although he is not, in fact, a rock performer but a "hit-man," a killer who is king of a syndicate in an elaborate futuristic version of an intergalactic gang war. Hoss's image is created and maintained by a group of fantastic followers: Becky, Hoss's consort who will stereotypically nurture, then betray him; Star-Man, a silver-suited astrology expert who reads Hoss's chart; Galactic Jack, a disc jockey who charts Hoss's course; Cheyenne, a contemporary cowboy, Hoss's driver. These disciples keep Hoss within the rules of the "game" which are stringently established and maintained by a group of enigmatic Keepers.

As the play opens Hoss has grown restless in his conformity to the rules and threatens to strike his next mark without waiting for the charts to signal the appropriate time. His retainers try to placate him, to keep him on the "inside" of the game as he tries to move "outside" into the world. His gang warns him that the outside is all locked up with rules set forth by other syndicates and that he would no longer recognize the world as he remembers it. Becky cautions him that going against the code will cause him to be dismissed from the game. But Hoss has begun to struggle against the confinement of an image imposed by his past. Becky reminds him that in a world kept and ruled by the code of the Keepers, it is suicidal to follow one's own nature. "That is what we saved you from," she tells him, "your nature . . . we molded and shaped you and sharpened you down to perfection because we saw in you a true genius killer." But Hoss insists, "The game can't contain a true genius. We don't have the whole picture" (p. 69).

Thus an opposition is established between nature and artifice as Hoss slowly apprehends his own fraudulent role in an elaborately constructed game. Like a character in a poorly made play who is squeezed and molded to' answer to the needs of an artificial structure, Hoss's action is determined by a set of rules drawn up by absent authors. Hoss is a character who strives to move outside of the frame of this picture into the "total picture," off the stage and into life. Shepard loads the dialogue with language that refers us to the theatrical nature of the action. To insure that an audience responds to the broader implications of the characters' words and their metaphorical nature, Shepard frequently changes the idiom in which the concept is presented. For example, Hoss suddenly exchanges his rock-and-roll rhetoric for the language of an oldtime cowboy: "The West is mine. I could even take on the Keepers. I'll live outside the fucking law altogether" (p. 75). A moment later he is speaking in the style of a 1920's gangster.

The tension between the ideas of "inside" and "outside" the game within the fictive reality of the play neatly parallels an audience's conceptual balance between onstage and offstage. This parallel is everywhere intensified in the language of the play, which enforces the opposition between fantasy and reality, and by the particular circumstance of the central character who performs his many roles in an unlocalized, and fantastically unreal, setting. Hoss is never allowed to leave the stage or cease performing and he is even made to believe that no world exists outside his private kingdom. Temporal and spatial fixity are deliberately disrupted by the language and dress of all the characters who represent noncontiguous historical periods. When Hoss tries to persuade Cheyenne to help him move outside the game, the latter replies, "the critics won't like it" (p. 76), powerfully reinforcing the metadramatic quality of the play. A major turning point for Hoss occurs when finally, having acknowledged his role as a performer, he discovers that there is no audience—he has been playing to an empty house. As he prepares for his last act, the showdown with Crow, Hoss refers to himself as a "star." He asks his opponent:

> . . . first I wanna find out how the Gypsy killers feature the stars. Like me, How do I come off? Are we playin' to a packed house like the Keepers all say?
>
> *Crow cackles*: Image shots are blown man.
>
> *Hoss replies*: You mean we're just ignored? Nobody's payin' attention? We're playing in a vacuum? All these years? All the kills and no one's watching?
>
> *Crow informs him*: . . . watching takes a side seat. Outside. The Game hammered the outside. (p. 91–92)

Hoss's worst fears have been realized as he recognizes: "This is incredible. It's just like I thought. The Outside is the Inside now" (p. 92). The interior/exterior duality, within Hoss's character and in the play's external world, is projected further onto the audience as representatives of the "Outside," whereas the play is the "Inside." In the La Mama production Hoss often spoke directly to the audience and peered out over the footlights as if he were trying to see into the world beyond the stage. This gesture brought the audience into personal proximity with the world of Shepard's play more powerfully than any direct physical contact. Shepard's recurrent exploration of entrapment and the various paths to liberation, almost always leading his heroes in a circle from prison to prison, is profoundly wedded to his concept of dramatic performance as a metaphor for existence. It is thus in the space between the tenor and vehicle of the world as stage metaphor, the "Ur-metaphor" for the theatre, that the action of *The Tooth of Crime* takes place. Shepard's plays relentlessly pursue reality through metaphor while demonstrating a painful longing to reconcile the basic distinctions between life and the reality of art. Hoss's need to integrate past self-images with the phases in his present state of becoming mirrors the structural movement towards a reconciliation of art and life. Theatre as metaphor is then the obvious and appropriate vehicle for Shepard to explore his hero's

ontology. Bruce Wilshire effectively describes the primacy of
the world as stage for dramatic artists:

There is a metaphorical reality expressed in theatrical and theatre-like
terms that is at least as basic as distinctions which we typically tend
to speak of as the most basic of all: subject and object, self and others,
offstage and onstage. These distinctions . . . are awash in the metaphorical and presuppose it.[39]

When the tenuous balance between onstage and offstage top-
ples, role-playing becomes inseparable from identity.

Since Hoss recognizes his world as a stage, his action determined in the way that an actor is bound by a script, he realizes
that all he has left is an image to preserve. The game then
becomes a "style match," and though Hoss tenaciously clings
to a belief in his own authenticity ("You ain't suckin' me into
jive rhythms . . . I got my patterns. I'm my own man. Original," he warns Crow, p. 103), he is fated to lose to this man of
the future who is a "master adapter," a genius actor whose
"image is [his] survival kit" (p. 111). Crow's song has the re-
frain, "I believe in my mask—the man I made up is me" (p. 94).
Crow will win the style match because he is capable of adopting roles with amazing speed and facility. He assumes Hoss's
language patterns and gestures in a matter of minutes. But most
important, Crow believes that the game, the play, and his mask
are real. Crow unites his life with his art (in this case, his performance), and embraces a plurality of selves, as opposed to
the singular self-image that confines Hoss. Hoss, on the other
hand, perceives the game as artifice, the styles as roles, and
himself as an unwilling actor. At one point in the duel of words
Hoss cries out, "Can the music. This ain't Broadway" (p. 100).
But ironically, the nature of the action is wholly theatrical, and
Hoss's recognition has come too late. Even the style match is
fixed and the referee biased in favor of Crow. Hoss tries to
make the match real; he wants to play "naked," to "strip this
down to what's necessary," but Crow only laughs and queries,
"Necessity?" (p. 100). "Necessity" is against the code, the ref-
eree tells Hoss. After losing the match and killing the referee,
Hoss pursues one last desperate attempt to survive. He pleads

with Crow to teach him his style, but Hoss has lost the capacity for role-playing that comes so easily to his usurper. Without this essential skill, Hoss has become thoroughly vulnerable to Crow, who never loses his protean attributes. Hoss has been exposed; he no longer has "a heart that the tooth of crime cannot wound."[40] With Crow's assistance Hoss conjures an image of his former self:

" . . . a true killer . . . true to his heart. Everything's whole and unshakable. He knows his own fate . . . Trusts every action to be what it is . . . Lives by a code . . . Speaks the truth without trying . . . Can't do anything false. . . . " (p. 109)

As the image fades Hoss collapses, screaming "It Ain't Me, It Ain't Me!" (p. 110). Without a "self" (he told Becky earlier in the play that they would both be "O.K." if they had a "self"), Hoss believes that he has no role to perform, so the only gesture left for him is suicide. "Stand back and watch some true style," he tells Crow, as he places the revolver in his mouth. Even Crow, the visionary adapter, appreciates the authenticity of Hoss's last gesture, "the genius mark." In a stage direction, Shepard cautions that Hoss's suicide should appear as natural as possible. It should not be performed in slow motion or accompanied by any "jive theatrical gimmicks" (p. 111). Shepard obviously would not want Hoss's final action to be performed in a nonrealistic manner because with this act, his character has broken the code, stepped off the stage and out of his role, and reestablished the authenticity of action. Hoss's last act is a desperate attempt to escape from the prison of his own self-concept (the inside) and the external world that is governed by the master illusionists (the outside) represented by Crow. Self-destruction becomes his only route to freedom, the only act he can execute to affirm a personal sense of self and reality in opposition to the determinate structure that everywhere blocks his route to authenticity in this metatheatrical play.

Shepard wrote *The Tooth of Crime* while he was living in England, but the most controversial production was undertaken by Richard Schechner's New York Performance Group. Schechner's notes as director, his correspondence with the playwright, and Shepard's reaction to the production together reveal some interesting information about the author's design and intentions for the play as well as reinforcing the centrality of the world as stage metaphor. Schechner's Performance Group is undoubtedly the single most outstanding example in the American theatre of an ensemble that practiced in the anti-illusionistic tradition. The Performance Group's experiments were directed toward breaking down the fundamental distinctions between performers, directors, playwrights, and audiences who, in Schechner's words, can now (after the triumphant anti-literary revolution in the theatre of the fifties and sixties) "watch, collaborate, participate, influence, and even dominate performances."[41] Schechner discovered in *The Tooth of Crime* a play "about performing and about techniques which The Performance Group [had] helped develop."[42] Schechner also draws attention to Shepard's obvious concern "with the different images people wear like masks; and also the contrasts between the styles of one era versus the styles of another."[43] It would seem then that the playwright and director would enjoy a felicitous working relationship, the latter so apparently expressing a sound understanding of the intentions of the former. But Shepard relinquished his script with a great deal of reluctance, fearing, among other things, "that the play will become over-physicalized and the language will fall into the background."[44] Nevertheless, he allowed the production to proceed; and given his penchant for scrutinizing the complexities of the "world-as-stage" metaphor, he curiously objected strongly to Schechner's use of performance space which did not separate the actors from the audience. More understandable was his objection to Schechner's decision to eliminate the songs from the production. These two criticisms are closely related and quite telling in regard to Shepard's theory of performance.

In addition to the obvious use of rock-and-roll to create an atmosphere of highly charged passion, violence, and driving force, the music is intimately connected to the structure of Shepard's play as point and counterpoint. Shepard uses music in at least seven of his plays, and each time the music serves an intricate, integrated function. As Toby Zinman points out, "it is not that there is music *in* the plays, or that it is added as some decorative device, but music seems to inform every aspect of this theatrical environment."[45] The music in *The Tooth of Crime* has much in common with Bertolt Brecht's conception of the *Verfremdungseffekt*—the music is meant to interrupt and comment upon the action of the play. It is a technique designed to insure that an audience is emotionally and aesthetically distanced from the action of the drama. Shepard wanted his music in *The Tooth of Crime* to function as momentary recesses during which the audience could affectively respond to the play's action.[46] Brecht would of course insist that his audience comment intellectually on the action; nevertheless, both dramatists insist upon the need for aesthetic distance. Clearly the effect of such a technique is opposed to Schechner's attempt to annihilate the boundaries between the play and the audience. Shepard felt that Schechner's production violated his intentions for *The Tooth of Crime*. He told the interviewer, "I think he [Schechner] is lost . . . in a certain area of experimentation which is valid for him."[47] Obviously Schechner's theory of performance was not valid for Shepard. Shepard's gradual movement away from anti-literary texts and anti-illusionistic techniques becomes apparent in his outspoken objections to the Performance Group's interpretation of *The Tooth of Crime*. Furthermore, and finally much more significantly, Shepard's transition is evident in the form and content of the play itself.

In his comments on the play, Shepard held fast to the traditional concept of a text in which language dictates certain actions and gestures. Moreover, Shepard objected strongly to the whole idea of a performance style that eliminated the boundaries between the play and the audience. He referred to the then current practice of environmental theatre in New York as a myth "that in order to be actively participating in the event they are watching, they [the audience] have to be physically sloshed into something, which isn't true at all."[48] He lampooned the production that attempts to enhance an audience's experience by having "spaghetti thrown all over them" and concluded that such practices might, in fact, cause an audience to become defensive and detract from their ability to appreciate the action of a play.

Schechner's methods were by no means simple theatrical

gimmicks. A strong and viable theory underlay such methods of production; at its heart was the belief in the theatrical event as a communal creation and experience. But along with the Performance Group's techniques came a shortening of aesthetic distance resulting in a deliberate merging of the world and the stage. In *The Tooth of Crime*, Shepard's hero suffers precisely from a coalescence of the world and stage. The particular nature of Shepard's criticism of the production indicates that the Performance Group violated the content or thought of the play. In other words, if we regard the performance as the final form of the play, the Schechner production failed to integrate the form and content of *The Tooth of Crime*.

I have argued that Hoss's progress in the play follows a movement from ignorance of his own role as a performer, a puppet for those whom he believes to be his subordinates, to the realization that his image is an artifice and that he has neglected his own changing nature for a singular image others have dictated for him. Confined to a game he does not fully understand, Hoss plays out his role until he falls victim to a younger, more flexible actor. On one level *The Tooth of Crime* is thus a ritual reenactment of the Ur-myth of the year-god, the hero or king who engages in a sacred combat with his rival and is overcome to make way for a new order.[49] Hoss is the sacrificed scapegoat in the classical paradigm.

On another level, this hero's particular failure is his inability to differentiate between theatrical and genuine action. Hoss does not know the difference between play and reality; thus, the game, the "inside," becomes his prison. Like Pirandello's Henry IV, Hoss awakens from his onstage stupor to discover that he is trapped in his role. Escape is impossible, for the "outside" has become the "inside"; his world is a stage and he has only one role left to play. As he says, "I'm pulled and pushed around from one image to another. Nothin' takes a solid form" (p. 105). Thus, Shepard shows us the perilous end of a character who loses his perspective by believing in the reality of play. The Performance Group's production placed the audience precariously close to the actors and eliminated Shepard's distancing devices. By doing so, they upset the dichotomy between theatrical reality and the external world that *The Tooth of Crime* criticizes. Since *The Tooth of Crime* demonstrates the pain of a failed integration, a performance style that seeks to reconcile the world and the stage would not complement the play's theme.

The Tooth of Crime represents a major departure for Shepard. As the play closes, Crow is in power and Hoss's former followers creep onto the stage to celebrate their new leader like the chorus in a Greek tragedy that laments or rejoices the establishment of a new order. Cheyenne's loyalty to his former boss causes Crow to reject his services, but the rest of the gang accept the usurpation as a perennial and inevitable experience. Nevertheless, Shepard finally has a hero who rejects a theatrical life and a singular image for another reality. Hoss is even willing to take his own life to demonstrate the genuineness of gesture as he clings to his belief that life must exist outside the game.

When Hoss becomes conscious of the false images that define himself and his world, he finds existence intolerable and suicide is the only means of escape. Shepard's criticism of the world is implicit in the form of *The Tooth of Crime*; but the mythic undertones in the play do not succeed in elevating Hoss to archetypal proportions. Nor does *The Tooth of Crime* clearly articulate a transformation from a monistic to a pluralistic metaphysic, although Crow's succession is suggestive of that process. Hoss's destiny still seems to fulfill a particular pattern rather than represent a universal condition. Raymond Williams discusses the phase that succeeded expressionism, "still deeply connected," but a development "in which dramatists tried to make [the implicit criticism of the world] explicit, by a new variation of form, requiring new conventions."[50] The succeeding phase takes the form we now call "absurdism"—"a total criticism of the possibility of a knowable world."[51]

ACTION

In *Action* (1975) Shepard presents four characters adrift in a world without references exploring the possibilities and limitations of performance and action.

In this play Shepard examines the ability to act without conscious purpose, a central precept in the absurdist tradition. The

play's four characters, Lupe, Liza, Shooter, and Jeep, occupy a
space sparsely furnished with the minimal images of a home:
a plain board table set with a simple place setting for four, a
pot of coffee in the table's center, a clothesline attached to the
sides of the stage by a pulley. Upstage center, a small Christ-
mas tree with blinking lights barely illuminates the otherwise
darkened stage. The holiday turkey that Liza prepares lacks the
customary trimmings and may well be their last meal. They are
fortunate, in fact, to have the meal, for they have seen ahead
into some unexplained crisis and raised their own turkey.[52]
Having survived the crisis, the characters must now recreate
the world. Shooter defines their motivation as a search for "a
way of being with everyone," and describes the method: "You
find out what's expected of you. You act yourself out" (p. 21).
The plot of *Action* resembles a rehearsal; the audience's experience is, in fact, much like observing a dramatic work in process. As a critic attending a rehearsal of George Ferencz's production of a Shepard trilogy at La Mama, Toby Zinman describes
his experience: "Watching a rehearsal, then, is like watching
life itself. The actors are searching for ways to be, for suitable
ways to express their characters' existence."[53] In *Action* Shepard uses the rehearsal as a metaphor for becoming, once again
fusing method and content in his vehicle of expression.

The characters have little memory of the world that existed
before they came together in this semblance of a home. Outside these four walls, there is no assurance that a world even
exists. Their home is not a refuge, for a profound sense of insecurity pervades their existence. Shooter reminds the group
that their home really offers little shelter: "It's still dangerous.
Anything could happen. Any move is possible" (p. 20). These
four people may be the last survivors of a holocaust, confronting a vast emptiness, confined, isolated, waiting to be born.
Jeep's first words reveal his ontological crisis and establish the
necessity for self-creation in a world without references that
informs the dramatic action: "I'm looking forward to uh—me.
The way I picture me" (p. 10).

Although Jeep retains a few images from the past—an ante-
lope on the prairie, Walt Whitman in an overcoat, himself sitting on a jeep with a gun in his hand—his "pictures" offer him

no references for action in the present. Jeep is content to hold these images in his mind to view time and again; he is committed to stasis. Shooter, on the other hand, craves experiment and exploration of the images. He tries to bring Jeep's picture of a dancing bear to life by acting it out, pulling his overcoat over his head and staggering around the stage like a bear on his hind legs, ignoring Jeep's protests, "Don't act it out, you're not the bear" (p. 12). But Shooter's performance leads to discovery. He learns that dancing bears feel off-balance, humiliated, as if they were performing for some unknown audience and confused about the purpose for their behavior. Like the dancing bear, Shepard's characters are self-conscious performers, vaguely aware of a division between what they do and who they are. Like Kent in *La Turista*, Shooter gradually becomes aware, as he enacts various roles, of the schism between an image of the self and the character who performs various actions. The action of the play represents these characters' attempts to unite a multiplicity of "selves" with action.

In order to make this ontological process visible, Shepard returns to the exploration of the essential theatrical metaphors. The women in the play, Lupe, and Liza, cling to the ritual of domestic duties, washing the dishes, preparing the meals, hanging the laundry. Their way of being in the world is defined by stereotyped action. Shepard rarely, if ever, gives us a woman who searches for authenticity. Freed of these domestic cares, Shepard's men face an ominous void in which they must authenticate themselves through action. Shooter and Jeep have no prepared script. Confronting their own egos across an empty space, they must attempt to define themselves by improvising, creating their own reality from moment to moment.

Shepard has created a situation for his characters that approximates his own as a playwright. Shooter and Jeep must "author" themselves, and thus the action of the play mimics the process of creating a dramatic structure. Such perilous freedom and responsibility paralyzes the characters. Jeep can find no motivation for action within himself. Seeking an author/director to endow him with a purpose, he asks Shooter, "Could you create some reason for me to move? Some justification for me to find myself somewhere else?" (p. 31). When

Jeep does attempt to act, he sees himself as an actor, not as a fully developed character, and he sees his movements as pretense. He has a picture of himself "that grew and grew until it came up against how [he] really was," and he explodes, unable to tolerate the conflict between his "actions" and the image (p. 16).

Further evidence of the metatheatrical nature of the drama is evident in the characters' awareness of an omnipresent, but detached, eye that watches them. Lupe dances a soft shoe, brazenly imitating the dance performed by the men earlier in the play. Dejected by Jeep's criticism of her performance, she stops and says that she did not want to continue because it made her feel "funny" to talk about it while she was actually performing, "like somebody was watching [her]. Judging [her]. Sort of making an evaluation" (p. 15). Jeep is also disturbed by the difference he perceives between actions that are performed publicly and privately. When Shooter tips over the armchair in which he had been sitting, concealing himself under it from the audience, Jeep asks him: "If you were alone would you have done that?" And Shooter replies: "I'm at my wit's end. The whole world could disappear" (p. 33). The world, for Shooter, is a projection of his own consciousness; when he "disappears" the world dissolves with him. Unable to define the self without communal references, Lupe and Jeep ask: "What's a community?" (p. 27). But no one can answer.

Shepard's play begins at a starting point that defines much of twentieth-century poetry. In his introduction to *Poets of Reality*, Hillis Miller defines one aspect of the thought that informs the poetry of this century: "By separating his subjectivity from everything but itself, . . . the ego has put everything in doubt, and has defined all outside itself as the object of his thinking power." The result is nihilism, "the nothingness of consciousness when consciousness becomes the foundation of everything."[54] Unlike Stu in *Chicago*, who was undisturbed by the absence of an objective world, Shooter and Jeep are painfully imprisoned by their own subjectivity. Like Beckett's characters who consistently seek an audience, the characters in *Action* wish to be recognized by others, but are unable to create a connection. They are disturbed by impressions of false causality as we see when Jeep improbably produces a dead fish from a bucket of water, and Shooter, who is standing on his armchair, makes Jeep promise not to think that he is afraid of fish. When Jeep hurls back, "I'm not thinking about you!" (p. 31), both men freeze in their respective positions. They are unable to act without the awareness and recognition of the other. Beckett's Estragon says to Vladimir: "We always find something . . . to give us the impression that we exist."[55] But Shepard's characters are even less hopeful. Isolated within their own consciousness, they finally cannot even be certain that they exist.

The objective world remains only in broken images, Jeep's "pictures"; Jeep and Shooter's objective is to reunite the fragments. Although they are unable to define their existential dilemma directly, Shooter represents it metaphorically in a monologue delivered directly to the audience. He tells the story of moths who were tormented by longing for a candle they could see in a distant window. Two messengers were sent to gather information about the light but were driven back by the heat. A third moth approached the light and, filled with love for it, threw himself on the flame, allowing it to consume him as they became one. The leader of the moths observed the union and recognized that the moth had gained knowledge but could not pass along his new understanding to others. The other moths envied the third moth's knowledge, but feared the self-consuming action that is necessary to gain such understanding. The story posits a tension between freedom, which implies ignorance and alienation, and commitment, which leads to the loss of the self.

Again Shepard's characters are faced with a dilemma similar to that of Beckett's characters, who must choose between isolation and attachment. J. R. Moore describes this dominant problem in Beckett's plays: "To be or not to be detached. Complete detachment is solipsistic insanity. Complete engagement would also be madness, like holding your hand over the flame from a gas burner."[56] Shooter's monologue shows us the fate of the moth who opts for total engagement, and he himself will experiment with the possibility of total detachment by isolating

himself in his armchair where he vows to remain forever so
that "the world can't touch [him]" (p. 25). Now it is Shooter,
the man who earlier wanted to act out Jeep's static pictures,
who commits himself to stasis. By refusing to act, Shooter thinks
that he is secure from the dangers that accompany a commitment to the world. But his sense of security is transient, and
he soon discovers that by isolating himself he has, in fact, made
a choice that is as frightening as freedom. Although he remains
true to his commitment, he soon grows restless and finally
panics: "I couldn't stay here Forever! I don't know what possessed me" (p. 33). Nevertheless, he remains in the chair until
the end of the play, convinced that worse things could happen.
Before he confined himself to the chair, Shooter was paralyzed
by the awesomeness of his own freedom and responsibility;
now he dreads his surrender to dependency. He is afraid that
he might have disappeared. "Maybe I'm gone," he tells Jeep.
However, Shooter still needs someone to verify his absence, a
reference. "Is there anyone to verify? To check it out?" he asks
Jeep, who has also become consciously aware of his own lack
of references: "I got no references for this. Suddenly it's shifted"
(p. 35).

A tentative community is established between the two men
as they share their feelings of emptiness and isolation. Jeep
responds to Shooter's request for a "clue" to their mutual dilemma by recalling the first time in his life when he recognized
his "true position": "I was in the world . . . up for grabs . . .
being taken away by something bigger. . . . " (p. 36). As Jeep's
memory returns, he begins to acquire some sense of himself
and his relationship to the world. He recalls entering a "new
world," which he likens to a prison—cement walls, no window. And then the anxiety would overwhelm him with "a
sweeping kind of terror." He would be unable to move, but
inside "something would leap like it was trying to escape . . .
an absolutely helpless leap," because he knew there was no
possible way of getting out (p. 37). As Jeep describes his experience, Shepard directs the actor to begin moving about the
stage "as if the words animate him . . . as though the space is
the cell he is talking about, *not* as though he's recalling a past

experience but rather that he is attempting his own escape *from the space he's playing in"* (p. 37). Shepard clearly wishes to emphasize here the correlation between an actor's peculiar dual awareness as actor and character, and the fundamental ontological division between self-images and actions.

Gerry McCarthy has worked out the development of the theatre metaphor that informs the action of this play. He calls attention to this moment when Jeep's speech "brings the states of understanding in imagined past events to bear upon the situation the actor finds himself in"[57] which he has previously defined as "moments *in extremis* when the actor is deserted by his technique and is most acutely aware of his own identity."[58] The double awareness of the actor, as a person who performs for others by enacting a role created by a playwright, and as an individual who develops a concept of self through the roles he or she plays onstage, is critical to an understanding of the thought that informs Shepard's drama. For not only do the actors experience this dual consciousness, they also represent it as mirrors of contemporary consciousness. Stanislavskian actors *become* the character they enact, losing themselves in the virtual self offered by the role. When the performance ends, the actor abandons the mask. Shepard's actors, however, are assigned the task of performing a role while simultaneously retaining an awareness of their private selves. Bonnie Marranca describes Shepard's method succinctly: "What usually happens in the theatre is that the actor is given the opportunity to be a character. Shepard reverses the practice by giving his characters the chance to be performers."[59] In *Action*, Shepard shows us the dilemma of characters who are *condemned* to being performers, confronted with the awesome responsibility of filling the empty space.

In his final monologue, Jeep describes the existential anxiety that grips all of the characters in the play: the feeling of dread produced by the vague awareness of a hostile outside force—"I knew I was threatened both ways, Inside and Out"; and the "other" that performs—"I was stalking myself"; the feeling of helplessness in a world without references—"I had no references for this"; and the concomitant feeling of purposelessness and the inability to control their world—"everything disappeared. I had no idea of what the world was. I had no idea how I got there or why or who did it" (p. 38). As the other characters perfunctorily perform actions they have routinely adopted, Jeep stands motionless as the stage darkens, quietly repeating his revelation: "I knew that even if I got out it would be like this. No escape. That's it. No escape" (p. 38).

Jeep's monologue recalls the final image in *La Turista*, Kent's absolutely helpless leap through the upstage wall. Both plays end in futility and despair. Shooter and Jeep are like Camus's stranger, existing in a universe "suddenly deprived of all illusions and light . . . irremedial exiles, deprived of memories of a lost homeland . . . and lacking the hope of a promised land to come."[60] They play out in images "the divorce between man and his life, the actor and his setting."[61]

Although the metaphysical solitude that is at the heart of an absurdist vision informs the action of Shepard's play, *Action* tentatively affirms some hope for the human condition. Even though Shooter, Jeep, and Lupe cannot define the word "community," they acknowledge some mutual understanding of the concept, and Shooter goes so far as to suggest: "I think we're beginning to get it [a sense of community] a little. To get it back. I mean you can feel it even in the dead of winter. Sort of everybody helping each other out" (p. 27).

At this point in Shepard's development, he could have continued to present the anguish of people isolated in a purposeless world, but this would have been to accept the ultimate inability of meaningful human action. Shepard chose instead to continue a search for meaning by creating dramatic structures that explore human relationships and the external structures that impose isolation and anxiety. In his next five plays Shepard abandons the expressionistic form that "uses the stage physically to realize inner images," and turns toward naturalism, the form that draws "much of its force from the physical existence of an unacceptable world, and from the presence in it of others, in the same dimension, with whom the attempt at a common understanding, a common recognition, must continue to be made."[62] Shepard begins his search with the family.

NOTES

1. Pete Hamill, "The New American Hero," an interview with Sam Shepard, *New York* (Dec. 1983), p. 98.

2. Sam Shepard, "Visualization, Language, and the Inner Library," in *Drama Review*, 21, No. 4 (Dec. 1977), p. 50.

3. Irving Wardle, "Childlike," *London Times*, 3 April 1970, p. 13.

4. Patti Smith, "Sam Shepard: 9 Random Years (7 + 2)," in *Sam Shepard: Mad Dog Blues and Other Plays* (New York: Winter House, 1972), p. 155.

5. Hamill, p. 86.

6. Sam Shepard, *Cowboys #2* in *Mad Dog Blues and Other Plays*, p. 131. Subsequent references cited in the text.

7. Hamill, p. 98.

8. Ibid., p. 96.

9. Shepard, *Drama Review*, p. 53.

10. Antonin Artaud, *The Theatre and Its Double*, trans. Mary Caroline Richards (New York: Grove Press, 1958), p. 46.

11. Ross Wetzsteon, "Sam Shepard: Escape Artist," *The Partisan Review*, 49, No. 2 (1982), p. 256.

12. Luigi Pirandello, *Six Characters in Search of an Author*, in *Naked Masks: Five Plays by Luigi Pirandello* (New York: E. P. Dutton and Co., 1952), p. 276.

13. Kenneth Chubb, "Fruitful Difficulties of Directing Shepard," *Theatre Quarterly*, 4, No. 15 (Aug.–Oct. 1974), p. 18.

14. Ibid.

15. Shepard, *Drama Review*, p. 55.

16. Ibid., p. 50.

17. Ibid., p. 52.

18. Sam Shepard, *Chicago* in *Chicago and Other Plays* (New York: Urizen Books, 1967), p. 3. Subsequent references cited in the text.

19. Sam Shepard, "Notes to the Actors," in *Angel City and Other Plays* (New York: Urizen Books, 1976), p. 6.

20. August Strindberg, "Author's Note," trans. Elizabeth Sprigge (New York: Doubleday, 1955), p. 193. Strindberg describes the form of the play: "Time and space do not exist; on a slight groundwork of reality, imagination spins and weaves new patterns made up of memories, experiences, unfettered fancies, absurdities, and improvisations." The single consciousness of the dreamer alone gives shape and form to the dream.

21. Ralph Cook, "Notes on *Chicago*," in *Chicago and Other Plays*, p. 2.

22. Ibid.

23. Sam Shepard, *La Turista* in *Sam Shepard: Seven Plays* (New York: Bantam Books, 1981), p. 257. Subsequent references cited in the text.

24. Elizabeth Hardwick, introduction, *Four Two-Act Plays*, by Sam Shepard (New York: Urizen Books, 1970), pp. 12–13.

25. Ron Mottram, *Inner Landscapes: The Theatre of Sam Shepard* (Columbia, Mo.: University of Missouri Press, 1984), p. 43.

26. Wetzsteon, p. 255.

27. Gerald Weales, "The Transformations of Sam Shepard," in *American Dreams: The Imagination of Sam Shepard*, ed. Bonnie Marranca (New York: The Performing Arts Journal Press, 1981), p. 41.

28. Arthur Ganz, *Realms of the Self: Variations on a Theme in Modern Drama* (New York: New York University Press, 1980), p. 219.

29. Sam Shepard, *Drama Review*, p. 58.

30. Hardwick, p. 13.

31. Richard Poirier, *A World Elsewhere: The Place of Style in American Literature* (New York: Oxford University Press, 1966), p.:15.

32. Ibid.

33. See Shepard's comments to John Lion, "Rock 'n Roll Jesus with a Cowboy Mouth: Sam Shepard is the Inkblot of the '80s," *American Theatre*, 1, No. 1 (April 1984), p. 9.

34. Artaud, p. 153.

35. Eugene O'Neill, *Long Day's Journey Into Night* (New Haven: Yale University Press, 1956), p. 153.

36. Eugene O'Neill, letter to George Nathan, quoted by Joseph Wood Krutch, *The American Drama since 1918* (New York: George Braziller Inc., 1957), pp. 92–93.

37. Ruby Cohn, "The Word is My Shepard," in *New American Dramatists: 1960–1980* (New York: Grove Press, 1982), p. 181.

38. Sam Shepard, *The Tooth of Crime* in *Sam Shepard: Four Two-Act Plays* (New York: Urizen Books, 1974), pp. 64–65. Subsequent references cited in the text.

39. Bruce Wilshire, *Role-Playing and Identity: The Limits of Theatre as Metaphor* (Bloomington, Ind.: Indiana University Press, 1982), p. 244.

40. Cohn, p. 180.

41. Richard Schechner, "The Writer and the Performance Group: Rehearsing *The Tooth of Crime*," in *American Dreams*, p. 167.

42. Ibid., p. 164.

43. Ibid., p. 165.

44. Ibid., p. 167.

45. Toby Silverman Zinman, "Shepard Suite," *American Theatre*, 1, No. 8 (Dec. 1984), p. 16.

46. See Sam Shepard, "Metaphors, Mad Dogs, and Old-Time Cow-

boys," an interview with Kenneth Chubb et al., *Theatre Quarterly*, 4, No. 15 (1974), p. 12.

47. Ibid., p. 13.

48. Ibid.

49. See Cohn, "The Word is My Shepard."

50. Raymond Williams, *Drama from Ibsen to Brecht*, (New York: Penguin Books, 1981), p. 393.

51. Ibid., p. 394.

52. Sam Shepard, *Action* in *Action and The Unseen Hand* (London: Faber and Faber, 1975), p. 18. Subsequent references cited in the text.

53. Zinman, p. 15.

54. J. Hillis Miller, *Poets of Reality: Six Twentieth-Century Writers* (Cambridge, Mass.: The Belknap Press of Harvard University, 1965), p. 3.

55. Samuel Beckett, *Waiting for Godot* in *I Can't Go On, I'll Go On*, ed. Richard W. Seaver (New York: Grove Press, 1976), p. 444.

56. J. R. Moore, "Some Night Thoughts on Beckett," *The Massachusetts Review*, 8 (Summer 1967), p. 537.

57. Gerry McCarthy, " 'Acting It Out': Sam Shepard's *Action*," *Modern Drama* 24, No. 1 (March 1981), p. 11.

58. Ibid., p. 2.

59. Bonnie Marranca, "Alphabetical Shepard: The Play of Words," in *American Dreams*, p. 14.

60. Albert Camus, *The Myth of Sisyphus*, trans. Justin O'Brien (New York: Vintage Books, 1959), p. 5.

61. Ibid.

62. Williams, p. 392.

Figure 1. Ella (Kathy Baker) finds her son's pet lamb in the otherwise empty refrigerator, an emblem of the family's persistent hunger.
Photo by Allen Nomura from the San Francisco Magic Theatre's production of *Curse of the Starving Class*.

Figure 2. Shelly (Betsy Scott) looks back despondently at a transformed Vince (Barry Lane) who succeeds his grandfather in the role of family patriarch. Photo by Ron Blanchette from the San Francisco Magic Theatre's world premiere of *Buried Child*.

Figure 3. Lee (Jim Haynie) burns the pages of his screenplay in violent frustration while Austin defiantly displays one of his stolen toasters. Photo by Allen Nomura from the San Francisco Magic Theatre's production of *True West*.

Figure 4. May (Kathy Baker) confronts her half-brother and former lover Eddie (Ed Harris). Photo by R. Valentine Atkinson from the San Francisco Magic Theatre's production of *Fool for Love.*

IV

REALISM REVISITED

I'd like to try a whole different way of writing now, which is very stark and not so flashy and not full of a lot of mythic figures and everything, and try to scrape it down to the bone as much as possible.[1]

So responded Sam Shepard to an interviewer's question concerning his direction as a playwright in 1974. "Realism?" the interviewer replied, and Shepard conceded that it might be called realism, "but not the kind of realism where husbands and wives squabble and that kind of stuff."[2] A few years later Shepard wrote *Curse of the Starving Class* (1977), the first of four plays that assume a realistic form to explore familial themes. *Buried Child* (1978), *True West* (1980), and *Fool for Love* (1983) followed in quick succession. Shepard's quartet of domestic dramas has in common, with certain modifications, a linear construction, a cause and effect pattern, a symbolic use of tokens and stage objects, a consistency in characterization, a wedding of language and explicit meaning, an emphasis on the past as a powerful determinant of the present, and a continuity of action, all of the ingredients that are essential to a realistically structured play.

When Shepard turned to domestic realism in 1977, he no doubt disappointed many who saw in his work a revitalizing force in the American theatre, an answer, in part, to Richard Gilman's plea for "an articulated consciousness, one that spreads among the practitioners and invades the theatre . . . one that cannot help being heard no matter what its efficacy will be allowed to

be."[3] But Shepard's return to the form and content that have
characterized serious naturalism since its inception should not
be misinterpreted as a retreat to worn-out conventions and tired
traditions. In his own way, Shepard has given new life to the
inherited structures of the past in much the same way that Ibsen injected truth and substance into the lifeless conventions
of the well-made play. Shepard's venture into social and psychological realism and his adoption of the naturalistic form have
resulted in plays that demonstrate Raymond Williams's faith
that naturalistic drama can still be authentically made, "that
the trap of a room, of a street, from which a man looks at a
world that at once determines and is beyond him, should go
on being experienced, in comparable dramatic actions; that certain illusions hold, and can be replayed but newly experienced."[4]

The impulse to dramatize family relationships has been a part
of Shepard's work since he began writing. *The Rock Garden* appeared on the double bill with *Cowboys* at Theatre Genesis in
1964. This one-act play expresses Shepard's feelings about leaving his home in southern California.[5] The first scene of *The Rock
Garden* is a pantomime, a dumb show that serves as a prologue
to the play. A man sits reading a magazine at the dinner table
while his teenage son and daughter sit opposite one another
sipping milk. The lights black out when the girl drops her glass,
spilling the milk.

In scene 2, a woman lies in bed covered with blankets while
her teenage son watches her from his rocking chair. The mother
talks about "angels on horseback," a cookie made of marsh-
mallows toasted on crackers, and tells her son about his grandfather, a "funny" man who used to lock himself in the attic
with his cats, refusing to entertain the guests who called on
him. She notices how much her son physically resembles her
father. The boy answers her in monosyllables and leaves the
room intermittently, each time returning wearing another item
of clothing until he is fully dressed. While the boy is offstage,
a man wearing a hat and overcoat passes through the room,
exits, then returns wearing only his underclothes as the boy
had been dressed earlier in the scene. When the man occupies

the boy's rocking chair, he continues the conversation with the woman who does not notice the exchange of roles.

This symbolic action in *The Rock Garden* anticipates similar action in *Curse of the Starving Class, Buried Child*, and *True West*. In all of these plays Shepard is obsessed with the inexorable power of inheritance, physical and psychological, the inevitable power struggle between father and son, and the son's eventual usurpation of the father's role. The third scene in *The Rock Garden* serves as a precedent for another of Shepard's recurring subjects. In this scene the father and son discuss the renovation of a house and lawn and the father's plans for a rock garden, bigger and better than the one he has now. As the man recounts his dream, the boy experiences spells of narcolepsy. The scene ends when the boy interrupts his father, radically shifting the subject in a long monologue about sexual intercourse and orgasm which he graphically describes and finally demonstrates by ejaculating, an action that recalls the image of the spilled milk in the opening dumb show.

The Rock Garden is a one-act play of images that suggest the barrenness and sterility of the psychic life of the family, a banality that is terrifyingly passed blindly from generation to generation, broken in this play by the boy's spontaneous monologue, a linguistically fertile rebuttal to his father's description of the barren rock garden. The boy's yearning for physical intercourse serves as an antithesis to the vapid social intercourse of the family. The images, action, and language of *The Rock Garden*, then, serve as a prelude to Shepard's concern with the emptiness and sterility of the hallowed American family.

In 1974 Shepard resisted the suggestion of an interviewer who perceived a certain shift in his drama from the presentation of direct images to metaphorical representation.[6] The interviewer astutely noticed a difference between the earlier plays and *The Tooth of Crime*, the play that I have argued marks Shepard's transition from images of a theatrical reality to the metaphorical presentation of a world outside the stage. It is not, however, until the late 1970's that the change in form becomes immediately apparent.

In Shepard's naturalistic plays, common names are given to

the characters—Emma, Vince, Lee, Shelly, and May replace the fantastical Jeep, Kosmos, Crow, and Galactic Jack of the earlier plays. The characters in the later plays are defined by their place and circumstance rather than by creating their own set and scene. And the relationships between characters are readily discernible in the later plays by familial or professional ties. Shepard's parents, children, siblings, lawyers, movie producers, and priests are representatives of a society defined by occupations or biological ties.

Shepard also relinquishes the freedom of nonlinear progression, which he employed in the earlier plays. Time and space are fixed. The characters can only enter the past or future through memories or dreams; they cannot control the outside world through their own perceptions. The box set, then, appropriately confines the action in a claustrophobic environment. Before, Shepard had been concerned with the way in which the dramatic character as an individual determined scene and situation. In these later plays, Shepard begins to explore the way in which outside forces determine character, the characters' reactions to the restrictive environment, and the way in which their actions are controlled by the abstractions of society—class, income, profession.

Bonnie Marranca points out an essential difference between Shepard's earlier plays and the family quartet: "There are no performances in these later plays, because the characters are caught up in the world of Fate, Necessity. Performance is an ironic attitude, not a tragic one."[7] Following in the path of his American precursors, O'Neill, Miller, Williams, and Albee, Shepard has moved into the mainstream to examine the demise of the most sacred of American institutions, the family.

CURSE OF THE STARVING CLASS

Curse of the Starving Class takes place in the kitchen of a middle-class American home. As the play opens, Wesley, the son, cleans up the debris left by his father when he demolished the front door in a drunken fury. As Wesley methodically throws fragments of wood into a wheelbarrow (his action suggesting that this is not an uncommon occurrence in this "typical"

American family), his mother, Ella, enters wearing a pink bath-robe and fuzzy slippers. This opening image of destruction and the calm acceptance of violence suggests that Shepard's Tate family has already plummeted to the bottom of their long day's journey. The stage picture presents an image of chaos and vulnerability. The barrier that insulates the family from the menace of the outside world has been battered down, and the culprit is the father, who has reversed his role as protector and now represents a threatening intruder.

The isolated images, connected by simple juxtaposition in *The Rock Garden*, become part of a narrative framework in *Curse of the Starving Class*. The structure of the play, however, continues to rely to a large extent on images, like the opening one, that expand into symbolic expressions of the destructive and disintegrating familial bond. Shepard's hero in the play is Wesley, the son who strives to untangle the constrictive cords that at once bind the family together and threaten to cut off the lifeblood of the individuals. Shepard depicts the family as a paradoxical union—life–giving, nurturing, protective, destructive, inoperative, but above all necessary, inescapable.

The play takes shape around a slender narrative. Weston's repeated drunken forays and irresponsible spending have alienated his wife, Ella, who secretly plots with Taylor, her lawyer, to sell the run-down farmhouse and escape to Europe with her children. At the same time, Weston plans to sell the family home to pay off his debts to Slater and Emerson, two hit men who are ruthlessly extorting money from him. Emma, their daughter, absorbs herself in 4-H club activities and the everyday realities of a typical midwestern high school student. Secretly, however, she dreams of ways to escape from her unhealthy home life. In long monologues she expresses her fantasies, which tend toward traditionally masculine pursuits and have as their objective the power and freedom she believes would accompany their realization. The individual family members are aware of each other's plans to a limited extent; but they do not confront each other directly with their emotional reactions to the threatened abandonment. Emma, for example, imagines herself a mechanic in a one-pump gas station in Los Cerritos, the only person in town who can repair the broken-down car that limps into the station carrying her mother and Taylor, who Emma knows are planning to run away together. She takes advantage of their ignorance, in her dream, by replacing the car's engine with a rebuilt Volkswagon block and charging them double for labor. Her delight in this fantasy is largely due to the reversal of roles in which she inflicts upon her mother her own feelings of isolation, hopelessness, and abandonment.

Wesley's monologues reveal his dream of escaping to Alaska, a new frontier, an undiscovered country rich with possibilities. More practically, he tells Emma that he hopes his parents will leave one day and never return, leaving the farm for him to manage. In the meantime Wesley continues to work on the farm, hoping that cosmetic repairs will have some improving effect on the horror of his family's life. Each member of the Tate family lives in his or her private dream, hoping that one day the rest of the family will become part of the fantasy. But each of them resists the efforts of the others to incorporate them consciously into their plans. Emma and Wesley discount their mother's efforts to persuade them to run away with her to Europe. Emma scoffs at Wesley's vision of a new frontier; Wesley dismisses Emma's dreams as childish fantasies.

Rather than moving forward to resolve some action, the play focuses on the consciousness of the characters as revealed through storytelling, a technique not far removed from the isolated monologues of the earlier plays since none of the characters really listens to the others' narratives. But in accordance with the naturalistic framework, Shepard incorporates the monologue method into an apparent dialogue. The structure of the action is built on a pattern of rising intensity, but Shepard does not create the sense that the action of the characters will resolve in a conclusion. Rather, he creates a pattern of images that build upon each other, complementing and reinforcing the action of the play, finally leaving behind strict realism.

The central image in the play is hunger: the refrigerator is opened and pillaged by family members who argue over whose responsibility it is to replenish it. Shepard frequently uses the absence of food, or its frenzied consumption, to indicate spiritual starvation, notably in *Action* when the characters take their places around a sparsely decorated table to partake of what is, quite literally, a last supper. In *Curse of the Starving Class*, the Tates continuously deny that they are part of the starving class, but they are always hungry. Weston returns from the desert bearing an armload of artichokes that boil on the stove throughout most of the second act. Ella cooks the chicken that her daughter had been saving for a 4-H club demonstration. Weston prepares a huge double breakfast of ham and eggs which he devours after swearing off alcohol. Ella empties giant sacks of groceries into the refrigerator, yet it is always half empty. Wesley gorges himself on unprepared food that he eats directly out of the refrigerator, leaving bits and pieces of meat littering the floor as they fall from his overstuffed mouth. These actions reify the psychic starvation of the cursed family, despite their denial of membership in the class.

The "curse" of the title manifests itself in two different but related forms. Emma has just experienced her first menstrual period which her mother assures her is a normal physiological function. Then she tells Ella that swimming may cause her to bleed to death and refers to her condition as a "curse." Ella also defines the curse as an abstract force that invades and surrounds all of them, linking it to the onset of menstruation and reminding us of the burden of original sin:

"It comes onto us like nighttime. Everyday I can feel it. Every day I can see it coming. And it always comes. Repeats itself. It comes even when you do everything to stop it from coming. Even when you try to change it. And it goes back. Deep. It goes back and back to tiny little cells and genes. To atoms. To tiny little swimming things making up their minds without us. Plotting in the womb. Before that even. In the air. We're surrounded with it. . . . It goes forward too. We spread it. We pass it on. We inherit it and pass it down, and then pass it down again. It goes on and on like that without us."[8]

The curse controls from within and from without; it is both an internal biological and psychological structure and an insidious invader that penetrates the family's enclosure.

The hereditary curse described by Ella slowly overtakes Wesley as he begins to feel the personal habits of his father creeping up on him. In a crucial encounter between father and son in Act II, Weston tells Wesley that it is good for the son to recognize his father's "poison"; that he failed to recognize it in his own life until he "saw [himself] infected with it"(p. 168). Wesley asks what the poison is, but Weston cryptically replies that he will find out in the same way that you poison a coyote, by putting strychnine in the belly of a dead lamb. Wesley fails to understand his father's cryptic analogy and, like his father, will be unable to avoid the poison. From the beginning of the play Wesley has been keeping a lamb penned in the kitchen, trying to save the suffering animal from an infestation of maggots. Shortly after his father's warning, Wesley addresses the lamb: "Eat American lamb. Twenty million coyotes can't be wrong"; then he opens and shuts the refrigerator door repeating the familiar ritual. But he reassures the lamb:

"You're lucky I'm not really starving. You're lucky this is a civilized household. You're lucky it's not Korea and the rains are pouring through the cardboard walls and you're tied to a log in the mud and you're drenched to the bone and you're skinny and starving, but it makes no difference because someone's starving more than you. Someone's hungry. And his hunger takes him outside with a knife and slits your throat and eats you raw."(pp. 156–157)

Wesley avoids identification with the starving man of his monologue by shifting to an imagined time and place and from first to third person. Defensively he protests his own inability to destroy the innocent animal he has nurtured. But in this fantasy monologue Wesley begins, through projection, his transformation into the father. Shepard uses the monologue, the form of dramatic delivery closest to narrative, to convey Wesley's fantasy, since fantasy, as André Green points out, "is closer to a form of theatre in which a narrator describes an action occurring in a certain place, but in which, though he is not unconcerned, he does not himself take part."[9] Wesley's unrealistic monologue conveys the sense that he has been overtaken by a power beyond his control; soon he will enact the curse of the starving class.

In Act III the incipient oedipal configuration posed in the father/son/mother triad achieves full resonance when Wesley dresses in the filthy baseball cap, overcoat, and tennis shoes discarded by his father. His transformation is so complete that even Ella can no longer distinguish between her son and her husband. Ironically, Weston has had an epiphany and undergone a kind of transformation himself. He has been "reborn" while walking in the garden in the early morning, regaining his sense of communion with the land that he owns and becoming aware of the physical bond, the flesh and blood that binds the family together. He comes to realize that the family's "bodies were connected and [they] could never escape that. But [he] didn't feel like escaping. [He] felt like it was a good thing . . . to be connected by blood like that. That the family wasn't just a social thing. It was an animal thing. It was a reason of nature that we were all together under one roof" (p. 187). While Weston was undergoing this rebirth, Wesley was inheriting the curse of the father. Wesley enters the kitchen to greet his reborn father, who is horrified to find his son wearing his discarded clothes, and calmly announces that he has slaughtered the lamb for food. Still hungry, Wesley ravenously devours food from the refrigerator, groaning as half-eaten morsels fall from his mouth to the floor. Like the coyote that eats the poisoned entrails of the lamb, Wesley has come to carry the father's poisonous curse; his transformation cancels out the birth of hope and renewal momentarily embodied in Weston. The hungry aggression Wesley had hoped to elude or contain within the father as object has instead been transferred from father to son. This scene vividly dramatizes the son's inner struggle with the antagonist of Eros in Freud's earlier theory, the self-preservation instinct, colloquially "hunger."

In a recent review, Benedict Nightingale has described the family in Shepard's plays as "less a refuge than a trap that seduces . . . and its roots and traditions are also its curse, an inexorable handing over of loss from one generation to the next."[10] In a final image, Shepard powerfully conveys this seductive trap and the symbiotic nightmare of the family. The Tates' mutually destructive dependency on one another is figuratively conveyed in the story that Weston relates at the beginning of Act III. After his rebirth, and while he attends the lamb that his son keeps penned in the kitchen, Weston is re-

minded of an incident that occurred one day as he went about
the unpleasant but necessary task of castrating the spring rams.
A giant eagle cast its shadow over his work, suicidally diving
close to the ground in pursuit of "those fresh little remnants of
manlihood" (p. 184). Weston's own memories of his wartime
exploits as a B-49 bomber triggered in him a powerful identification with the eagle; and he found himself cheering in concert
with the eagle's daredevil antics. Weston refuses to complete
this narrative when Wesley unexpectedly enters the room.

At the end of the play, the sight of the dead lamb in her
kitchen awakens Ella's memory of the story she heard her husband repeat so often. Wesley, still dressed in his father's clothes,
helps his mother remember the details. Ella and Wesley cannot
face each other, but with their backs turned they alternate lines
to complete the story. A big tom cat comes, Ella remembers,
jumping on the roof to sniff at the "entrails"—she substitutes
the poisoned entrails of the lamb for the testes of the original
story. And the eagle returns, Wesley continues, snatching the
cat in its talons and carrying it away screaming into the air.
Ella stares at the lamb's carcass as she describes the mid-air
fight, the cat tearing the eagle's chest out, the eagle trying desperately to drop him, the cat clinging to the eagle even as he
tears his heart out because if he lets go he knows that death
will be sure and sudden. And as the eagle is torn apart in mid-
air, the two come crashing down to the earth together, inextri-
cably intertwined. "Both of them come crashing down. Like
one whole thing" (p. 201), Ella concludes as the lights fade
slowly to black.

The image in the concluding narrative represents the bond
of the family, the wife and children dependent upon the father, whose flight from responsibility carries the family with
him to destruction. They must cling to him in their helplessness, but their clutching destroys him and finally all of them
tumble down together fatally bound to each other by biological
chance, their destinies determined by their interdependence in
a bond that cannot be broken.

Although Wesley and his mother remain in their home at the
end of the play, little hope is offered as the play concludes with
the repetition of this violent, self-destructive image. Weston has

left for Mexico where he hopes to elude Slater and Emerson. We assume that Emma is killed in the car that Slater and Emerson blow up as a warning to Weston, for the last we see of her she is planning to steal her father's car to run away in. Some optimism exists in Ella's final recognition of Wesley, whom she has identified with her husband since the former's transformation. Wesley has perhaps symbolically destroyed his father by becoming him for a while and successfully passing through the stage to assert his own identity. Although there is no indication in Shepard's play that Wesley desires his mother, the oedipal theme clearly informs the father and son relationship. The curse that Ella describes is handed down from generation to generation in an inescapable pattern that consumes the entire family. The oedipal myth resonates in the play's final image. The eagle that greedily devours the testes carries away the tom cat that demands a share in the feast; but in order to destroy the eagle, the cat must sacrifice himself.

BURIED CHILD

In Shepard's next play, *Buried Child* (1978), he continues to focus on father and son relationships, this time examining three generations in a single family. Again Shepard works within an essentially naturalistic framework; but this play comes close to mocking the form. Jack Richardson comments on the peculiar blending of forms that Shepard achieves:

Somehow, Shepard manages to strike a balance between naturalistic detail and the wilder, more secret landscapes of being. He has found a way of maintaining a tension between the banal and the strange that gives his plays the quality of lucid dreams.[11]

Nowhere in the playwright's work is this convergence more apparent than in the Pulitzer prize–winning *Buried Child*, a play that on the surface appears wholly naturalistic, conceding to Zola's demand for "direct observation, accurate anatomy, acceptance and representation of what *exists*."[12] Shepard's play carefully sustains a realistic veneer, adhering almost formulaically to the familiar Ibsen/Strindberg brand of realism in theme and structure. The device of a fatal secret deeply hidden beneath the surface of a mundane domestic scene is gradually revealed through dialogue and action, the revelation resulting in a profound conflict that threatens permanent disruption of the normality and tranquillity of the domestic life of the family. As the catastrophe approaches, weighty significance is retrospectively attached to words and behavior that originally appeared without import. Dramatic irony magnifies the action of the drama as a final transvaluation, a moral and psychological upheaval, forever alters the perception and consciousness of characters and audience. In this familiar dramatic form, the structure of the plot is essentially a puzzle with each character in custody of clues that are part of the total picture, a picture that begins fragmented but will cohere as the action unfolds, forming a conceptually satisfying unity.

Ibsen may leave his characters and audience with an unresolved moral dilemma or with perplexing psychological ambiguities, but basic questions concerning the nature of past actions, and the identity and relationship of characters are revealed through an exchange of information. On the other hand, although in *Buried Child* Shepard intentionally sets up an audience to follow the tantalizing clues that he exhibits in an effort to integrate the fragments into an accommodating whole, he undercuts our expectations, frustrating our ability to resolve the action of the play realistically, allegorically, *or* symbolically. Our expectations for a realistic drama are immediately aroused by the initial *mise en scène*, the interior of a rather shabby middle–class American living room. Once highly successful midwestern farmowners, Halie and Dodge should now be reaping the rewards of their long struggle for comfort and security. Their family should have reached maturity, their sons a support for the aging parents. But Dodge has become a cynical, cantankerous old man who spends his days riveted to a blank television screen, gazing numbly from his confined space on the living room sofa where he surreptitiously sips from a whiskey bottle concealed beneath the cushions from the watchful eye of his nagging wife. Halie lives in a private world in her upstairs bedroom, a refuge cluttered with pictures from the past. From her window she claims to see the whole world passing by, but her interests are in refurbishing the past with glowing images of a blissful home life. Ansel, her son who died in the war, is an obsessive memory for Halie. She leaves her refuge only to seduce Father Dewis, the local minister who has promised to erect a statue in the town square in memory of Ansel, a monument commemorating his patriotism and status as an all-American athlete, a rifle in one hand and a basketball in the other. As the play opens we hear Halie calling down the stairs admonishing her husband who appears to have been long deaf to her complaints. She finally appears dressed in black, as much in mourning for herself as for her dead son.

Halie attempts to preserve the illusion of a happy and successful family, but her hopes are all in memory and even her remembrances are distorted. We discover, for example, that Ansel's "heroism" consisted of dying mysteriously in a motel room on his honeymoon before he had a chance to win any of the medals that his mother longed for. Halie's two living sons have failed in their potential and her expectations. Bradley, her youngest son, recklessly cut off his leg with a chain saw and is now psychopathologically bent on terrorizing his father. Tilden, the eldest son and a former all-American fullback, has returned to live with his parents after subsisting in Mexico for twenty years. Dull and confused, Tilden must be watched constantly like a demented child. Such is the family's situation when Vince, Tilden's son, arrives with his girlfriend Shelly to affirm his memories of a Norman Rockwell–poster past and to effect a reunion with his family after a six-year absence.

The arrival of characters whose ignorance due to absence provides the occasion for realistic exposition supports the already established anticipation of a naturalistic play. And indeed, Vince and Shelly's unforeseen appearance acts as a catalyst for a conflict that has long been dormant in the family. The family in *Buried Child* suffers from the tyranny of the past, an action performed decades ago, a truth half-told that threatens to explode their slender hold on normality, turning their tedious day-to-day existence into a nightmare. The young couple are intruders who unwittingly force the discovery of the secret that binds the family together in a fearful union. Shelly serves as an objective presence, an outsider with no familial ties whose point of view provides an audience with a perspective from which they can judge the reality of this family's life. The offering of such an objective viewpoint is a new technique for Shepard, whose method in the past has been to present a myriad of distorted consciousnesses, each equally unreliable, producing a chaotic effect by denying his audience the ability to identify with a character who sees the disordered action of the play from the outside.

Shelly enters her boyfriend's childhood home prepared for a weekend of "turkey dinners and apple pie,"[13] a notion that reduces her to hysterical giggling. Composing herself finally, she enters to find Dodge passed out on the sofa with his head shaved and bleeding, the consequence of one of Bradley's terrorist acts. When Dodge awakens, he fails to recognize his grandson, Vince. Despite Vince's attempts to reassure Shelly that his grandfather must be ill, senile perhaps, Shelly immediately perceives something horribly amiss in the family, and she reacts with anxiety that is transferred to the audience. When Tilden, Vince's father, also fails to recognize his son, Shelly's reaction intensifies to terror and the action begins to take on a surreal quality.

From Vince and Shelly's point of view, there are three possible explanations for the failed recognition: Dodge may be senile and Tilden mentally impaired, an assumption that receives some support from the prior behavior of the two men. Second, Dodge and Tilden may be playing a cruel joke on Vince, an idea that occurs to Shelly in Act II when, alone with Dodge, she mentions that if they really do know Vince then the game they are playing is unfair. Finally, it is possible to conclude that Vince has arrived at the wrong house and mistaken the inhabitants for his father and grandfather, certainly the most unlikely interpretation but one that does cross Shelly's mind and understandably heightens her apprehension. Upon close examination, none of these explanations proves satisfactory within the conventions of realism. Tilden is convincingly portrayed as a mentally disturbed individual (he returned home from Mexico because he got "mixed up, couldn't figure anything out") and thus we might realistically accept his inability to recognize his son. But Dodge, though very old and ill, is lucid and crafty, only playing the senile grandfather when it suits the purpose of irritating his wife. Dodge could very well be capable of playing a cruel joke on Vince, but Tilden seems incapable of such a performance and the two men have had no opportunity to confer in a conspiracy given Vince's totally unexpected arrival. That the "joke" occurred to both men simultaneously is highly unlikely. As for the third possibility, Vince appears in every way a normal, well-balanced young man with no tendencies toward hallucination and no impairment of his sense perceptions. We are left, then, without a suitable explanation for the failed recognition that presents itself as the critical dramatic question of the play.

In earlier plays, Shepard has repeatedly posed the question of self-recognition and explored the nature of identity from the vantage point of social roles and the private self. As I have emphasized in my discussion of the earlier plays that pursue these questions, the open structure of expressionism has been used in its many variations as the form most conducive to the inward-turning, self-analytic theme. Now, however, Shepard is working with the themes of home, family, heredity, and environment; as he adopts the naturalistic frame he moves into the exploration of the self in relationship to others, the family representing the first encounter between the ego and the world. Vince is clearly on a quest to recover his past by verifying his memories. To fulfill his search for identity, Vince needs to justify his origins. However, the initial experience of his homecoming exactly reverses his anticipation since his father and grandfather refuse to acknowledge the bond of flesh and blood that unites them. *Buried Child* then begins with a rejection of one of the concluding statements of *Curse of the Starving Class*, the play that immediately precedes it. In the earlier play, Weston, the father, experiences a rebirth with the recognition that a bond of flesh and blood ties a family together in a union that, however discordant, cannot be dissevered. In *Buried Child*, the family attempts to repudiate the physical bond, but its inexorable power reaches from beyond the grave to claim them.

Despite the virtually incomprehensible behavior of Dodge and Tilden, we are still encouraged to search for realistic explanations as we respond to Vince's determined effort to force their

recognition. Vince can scarcely allow that his physical appearance has changed so drastically in six years as to render him
unrecognizable, but in desperation he admits the possibility and
begins performing tricks that he entertained them with as a
child, hoping that his youthful games will jar their memories.
His tricks eliciting no response, Vince sarcastically suggests that
perhaps he has committed some moral offense such as
"plung[ing] into sinful infatuation with the Alto Saxophone"
that may have caused his family to reject him (p. 97). Vince
thus posits two reasons, one physical, one moral, in a last attempt to alleviate his confusion and resulting distress. Both attempts fail, and Shelly, embarrassed by her boyfriend's pathetic bahavior, admonishes him: "Jesus Christ. They're not
gonna play. Can't you see that?" (p. 96). Shelly's comment re-
opens the possibility that Dodge and Tilden are in collusion,
sharing an understanding somehow connecteʋ ɩʋ the secret they
share, and Vince is an innocent victim of some sinister intent.
We are still, however, unable to discover a reason for the game;
indeed, the search for one will prove futile. Perhaps it is at this
point in the play's action that we should abandon the search,
for after all it appears that the realistic surface of the drama has
been irreparably cracked. Mel Gussow sees *Buried Child* as a
play demonstrating that "love and friendship are ties that can
be thicker than blood" and that "parents and children have to
'prove' themselves to earn their relationships."[14] But Gussow's
thematic speculation encourages us to fill in Shepard's deliberately unrealistic gaps. Much more instructively for an appreci-
ation of *Buried Child*, Gussow also alludes to Shepard's indebt-
edness in this play to the methods and techniques employed
by Harold Pinter, specifically in *The Homecoming* which is an
obvious forerunner. But Shepard's play also has strong affinities with Pinter's *The Caretaker*. The game that Dodge and Tilden play is as apparently unmotivated and unconscious as the
one Mick and Aston play on Davies in Pinter's play. The brothers in Pinter's play alternate between befriending the old man
and terrorizing him, primarily by undercutting Davies's most
simple perceptions and confounding his basic human expectations by engaging in unmotivated acts of brutality and sudden
shifts in character. Richard Schechner indicates the difficulty in

verifying Aston's "conscious cooperation with his brother in Davies' destruction," pointing to Aston's mental disorganization resulting from the electric shock treatment he received in order to be released from the hospital.[15] Shepard's Tilden and Dodge parallel Pinter's brothers in respect to their personalities as well: Dodge, like Mick, cruel and crafty; Tilden, like Aston, dull, laconic, mentally disturbed.

The influence of Pinter's *The Homecoming*, which Gussow mentions but does not elaborate on, is even more obvious. Vince and Shelly return home after a long absence just like Teddy and Ruth in Pinter's play. Dodge mistakes Shelly for a prostitute, just as Max accuses Teddy of "bringing a tart" into his home.[16] Both households are predominantly male, a father and two sons, though in Pinter's play the mother is dead whereas Halie is simply absent for most of the action in *Buried Child*. The obvious parallels begin to break down after the initial comparison, but the structural patterns of these plays continue to bear strong resemblances to each other. The women in both plays suffer a similar fate. Ruth in *The Homecoming* is marked by the family as a victim, but gains some measure of control by turning their threatening game into serious play. Teddy's family tries to degrade and humiliate Ruth, but she converts the stigma they impose on her into a profitable business venture. Shelly manages only bare survival by keeping herself busy with domestic duties, cutting and cooking carrots, making bouillon for Dodge, pacifying the men by offering them her rabbit coat. Pinter's Ruth becomes a prostitute for the men who abuse her; Shelly is victimized and symbolically raped by Bradley who forces her to stand passively with an open mouth into which he inserts his fingers. She has a moment of successful retaliation when she steals Bradley's wooden leg while he is sleeping, rendering him momentarily impotent. Shelly finally escapes from the madhouse when Vince returns not to rescue her but to reject her. In Pinter's play Teddy is rejected from the family who keeps his most "prized possession." Shepard's hero also loses the woman, but claims his power as heir to the ramshackle estate.

The ostensibly realistic structure is thus a perversion of naturalistic convention, an uncommon form in the American theatre, but following the pattern Schechner describes as essentially Pinteresque, "conceptual incompleteness, the conceptual world out of which the plays emerge . . . sparse, fragmented . . . no single rational frame to answer all the questions."[17] As in Pinter's plays, we never know why certain actions occur in *Buried Child*, and we are not meant to know. No intelligible pattern is disclosed behind the dissociated actions, confounding Zola's scientific method of observation, in itself far from an avant-garde stance since a whole movement in modern drama, beginning perhaps with Ibsen's *The Master Builder*, has been away from the belief in logical causality and the capacity for objectivity. But Shepard's play strikes us as radically different because of the convergence of the naturalistic form, cognitive and realistic, with disturbing action that exactly reverses an audience's expectations. Motives are left undiscovered; the past is revealed but fails to illuminate the present; character becomes increasingly disorganized and action unpredictable. The two antithetical forms jarringly combine to produce an uneasy, inexplicable action that taunts our ability to make our observations intelligible.

Shepard's play evokes an even more powerful frustration than Pinter's by suggesting another level of interpretation and then withdrawing it. While we are puzzling over the causes of and motivation for Dodge and Tilden's failure to recognize Vince, we are kept persistently aware of the other story, the secret of the buried child, which would seem to hold the final clue to the mystery. Just when Shelly, who becomes our only source of an objective viewpoint when Vince leaves her alone with his family, begins to accept the puzzling rejection of Vince and to overcome her fear of these mystifying strangers, Tilden reveals to her the family secret, "the secret buried treasure," the baby "they" had once, drowned by Dodge and buried in the garden.

The identity of the buried child, or Dodge's motivation for killing it, would seem to explain the bizarre behavior of the family. Although the child's origin remains a mystery, once again we are given a number of significant clues that appear to be leading toward an important recognition. The first allusion to the dead child occurs in Act I, scene 1, when Halie prepares to leave the house for her luncheon with Father Dewis. As she walks out the door, she reminds Dodge that their son Bradley will be coming over later in the day to give his father a haircut, an action that we later see brutally realized when Bradley shaves his father's head until it is cut and bleeding, suggesting displaced castration. Dodge reacts very violently to this announcement, insisting that Bradley has no right to enter the house, that he belongs in a "goddamn hog wallow" where he was born, and that Bradley is "*not* his flesh and blood." "My flesh and blood," Dodge tells Halie, the *only* progeny he openly claims as his own, "is buried in the back yard!" (p. 76).

In Act III, Dodge decides to reveal the whole story to Shelly. He tells her that the child was borne by Halie, a baby that came late in life after the couple had not been sleeping together for six years. He insinuates that Tilden fathered the child but "it [the baby] wanted to pretend that I was its father. She [Halie] wanted me to believe it. Even when everyone around us knew. Everyone. All our boys knew. Tilden knew . . . Tilden was the one who knew. Better than any of us" (p. 124). Halie's incestuous feelings for at least one of her sons have already been suggested in the first scene when she remembers the marriage of her dead son Ansel and the way he kissed her coldly as he left for his honeymoon. "He never used to kiss like that," she recalls, and expresses her repugnance about losing him to his wife: "Hating me and loving her!" (p. 74). When Dodge tells Shelly the story about the murdered infant, we read this first scene retrospectively with added significance, a familiar experience of realistic drama. But Shepard does not follow up with this neat convention, once again diverting our expectation. He could have intimated that the dead child was Halie and Ansel's, or even Bradley's, the son who fiercely protects his mother and despises his father. But the connection Shepard leads us to make does not suit the naturalistic framework. Instead, we are returned to the problem of Vince's identity. In Act II, when Tilden first encounters Vince, he denies being his father, but acknowledges, "I had a son once but we buried him" (p. 92), thus confirming his fatherhood of the dead child even though Dodge then insists that the child was born long before Tilden was born. Dodge's feeble retort is contrary to all the other evidence in the play and is thus easily dismissed.

Despite the conflicting stories, it appears that the two plots, the secret of the buried child and Vince's unresolved relationship with the family, are dependent upon each other and will merge into a determinate structure. We believe that Vince is Tilden's son; and we begin to suspect a connection between Vince and the buried child when he cries out in frustration: "How could they not recognize me? I'm their son" (p. 97). Although Tilden and Dodge are both in the room when Vince asks this question, significantly it is Dodge who answers: "You're no son of mine. I've had many sons in my day and you're not one of 'em" (p. 97). Given what we later discover about Halie's attempt to present her baby to the world as Dodge's own, and Dodge's passionate renunciation of the child, a connection between Vince and the "murdered" infant seems to be made here. One more detail is significantly omitted. No mention is ever made of Vince's mother or a wife or lover in Tilden's life. We do know that Tilden has been in Mexico for the past twenty years and that Vince is a young man in his twenties. We might then assume that Tilden fathered the child and went to Mexico to hide or escape after the child disappeared, and that Vince, the "buried" child, has returned after all this time to stir up the repressed fears and hostilities engendered by his birth, to awaken the family's memories, and to reclaim his lost inheritance.

Buried Child could then be read as a realistic drama fraught with psychological aberrations, not unlike Albee's *Who's Afraid of Virginia Woolf?* In Albee's play, George and Martha's son is a fantasy created to sustain a relationship built upon layers of illusion, with the imaginary child at the center of their fantasy life. Through the exorcistic games that form the center of the action, each fantasy is exposed until the final illusion that has been taboo in their violent destruction of one another's dreams is exposed, and George and Martha are forced to face the harsh reality of their relationship. Albee's play is based upon the stripping away of an imaginary existence. In Shepard's play we begin to suspect that the secret murder is fabricated by Dodge and accepted by the entire family as a way of coping with the unbearable truth of Vince's incestuous generation. Dodge and Tilden's refusal to acknowledge the biological bond with Vince is intelligible in this interpretation since they have buried him in their memories. His unexpected arrival understandably wreaks havoc on their psychic stability, and denial becomes the anticipated response.

In Act III, Dodge announces his impending death and proclaims his last will and testament, finally recognizing Vince who has returned after an all–night sojourn with his past, reviewing his heritage and seeing himself as unmistakably the last in a long lineage. Dodge acknowledges the young intruder as his own, proclaiming: "The house goes to my Grandson, Vincent" (p. 129). Dodge leaves his farming tools to Tilden, the tiller of the soil, but all other possessions are ordered piled in the desert in a heap to serve as his funeral pyre. Vince readily accepts the responsibility to carry on the family name and tradition as he takes command of the living space. Vince usurps Bradley and Tilden, chases Halie (who has finally returned from her overnight "luncheon" with Father Dewis) upstairs, and ignores Shelly who no longer recognizes him. His last act is to bury his grandfather's corpse with an old woolen blanket, placing Halie's roses on his chest, and positioning himself on the sofa in Dodge's place, arms folded behind his head, his body symmetrically mimicking the position of Dodge's corpse. This scene perfectly parallels the first as Halie's voice is heard calling down the stairs, "Dodge? Is that you Dodge" (p. 132). The drama appears to have come full circle, the buried child emerging to replace the father who murdered him. Like Wesley in *Curse*, Vince cannot transcend his past; the inexorable power of the patriarchy claims him.

In the final scene of the play Shepard powerfully reinforces this action with a remarkable image of the son's circular quest. Throughout the play Tilden has made several appearances on stage carrying corn and other vegetables that have mysteriously grown in the garden that Halie and Dodge claim has been barren for the last forty years. Despite his parents' refusal to believe that the garden has produced, Tilden patiently reaps the harvest from the ground, carrying in the plentiful produce. Now, at the end of the play, from her upstairs bedroom window Halie sees the corn growing. Astounded by the bounty, she remarks: "It's like a paradise out there. . . . A miracle" (p. 132). While Halie continues to exclaim over the crop, Tilden carries in his final armload from the garden, the skeleton of an infant wrapped in a muddy, rotten cloth. Here Shepard links the mother and son with agrarian rituals and creates a vivid theatrical correspondence between sexual union and natural fecundity as Tilden slowly climbs the stairs to deliver his child to its mother. Walking straight past Vince who lies motionless on the sofa, and paying no heed to his father's body, Tilden walks deliberately up the steps to deliver the child he has unearthed to its mother as she continues to rhapsodize about the paradise beneath her window in words that metaphorically allude to the resurrected child:

"You can't force a thing to grow. You can't interfere with it. . . . You just gotta wait 'til it pops up out of the ground. Tiny little shoot. All hairy and fragile. Strong though. Strong enough to break the earth even." (p. 132)

After forty years of lying dormant in the barren field, the crop planted by Dodge has suddenly burst from the ground, transforming the garden into a new Eden. But along with the bountiful crop, the family's "treasure" has also broken ground, the hideous crime fearfully imaged in the decayed corpse. Tilden, the one member of the family who is in touch with the fertile earth and in communion with the mysteries of nature, presents the tangible evidence of his family's grotesque past. Halie's tiny shoot that was trampled underground by Dodge before it had a chance to grow does indeed emerge strong, but in the person of Vince who returns radically altered. Determined to inherit the family estate, Vince terrorizes his family and takes over the position as head of the household. Yet it is the gentle nurturer Tilden, who cares for his offspring and tends the harvest, who performs the final action of the play. Doris Auerbach points out that *Buried Child* ends "like a miracle play with the symbol of the resurrection," and because Tilden carries the child upstairs to its mother, rather than to the dead patriarchal figure on stage, the play "leaves the audience with hope for a revitalized America, for one that nourishes its children and holds the promise of the American dream once again."[18]

Richard Gilman also sees hope in the final action of *Buried Child*: "the fantastic field is a metaphor for fecundity, of course, and at the same time works as a hope of future life against the bitter hidden truth which emerges at the end in the form of the murdered 'buried' child."[19] Nonetheless, Shepard's optimism is, at best, highly ambiguous in this play. As Bernard Weiner suggests, Vince is the real buried child of this play.[20] And much more clearly than even Wesley in *Curse of the Starving Class*, Vince inherits the patriarchal tendency toward power, domination, and violence best represented through his grandfather Dodge and uncle Bradley. The gentle Tilden does unearth his son and quietly carries his progeny upstairs to the mother, but the matriarchal lineage is presented passively and negatively in a number of ways. Halie's domain is offstage, unseen, and primarily a repository for the past. Her nurturing son is demented, impotent, and their mutual recognition of the garden's fertility is discarded as a source of sustenance. Finally, and most powerfully, the product of their union, though finally uncovered, is presented in the image of a disintegrating corpse, little more, in fact, than a muddy, rotten cloth. Vince, the buried child incarnate, like Oedipus, is a young man who tries to escape his destiny only to discover that he himself must excise the debilitating secret of his heritage. And in the process, like Oedipus, he discovers himself to be the source of the "plague" that pervades his people. But unlike Oedipus, who symbolically castrates himself through the displaced blinding and banishes himself from his homeland, Vince proudly asserts his newly discovered power and stays to dominate the home in his grandfather's stead. *Buried Child*'s ending is highly problematic. Has a healthy exorcism taken place or has a loathesome existence been portrayed that will continue in direful repetition? Shepard clearly has not resolved the issue as he continues to explore this crucial question.

TRUE WEST

In the third of Shepard's naturalistic dramas the playwright combines the disturbing, disparate elements of modern American existence into a powerful and convincing dramatic unity

that operates on multiple levels. *True West* (1980) pits the rugged frontier individualist against the urban socialite, a familiar
struggle first dramatized by William Vaughan Moody in *The
Great Divide* when the "effete self-conscious East met the rough
and open-hearted West."[21] From *Cowboys* to *True West* Shepard's dissenting voice has rebelled against the restrictions of
urban life and defiantly, often nostalgically, asserted the claims
of freedom and adventure embodied in the myth of the American West.

Before *True West*, Shepard had often modeled his heroes on
legendary figures in American Western mythology: in *The Unseen Hand* (1969) three cowboy brothers, Blue, Cisco, and Syc-
amore Morphan, are resurrected to save Willie (the Space Freak)
from the Silent Ones' "unseen hand" that oppresses him and
his people in Nogoland by curtailing their reasoning processes.
Willie believes that the cowboy brothers who died in the nineteenth century can render the technology and magic of the "Silent Ones" impotent. "You would be too real for their experience," he tells Blue Morphan.[22] In *The Unseen Hand* the legendary
characters from the old West have more reality than Shepard's
vision of the future and are shown to be sources of salvation
from the abstract powers that limit common humanity. In
Geography of a Horse Dreamer (1974) the gifted young dreamer Cody
is rescued from the kidnappers who exploit his talents when
his brothers Jasper and Jason, wearing well-used authentic Wy-
oming cowboy gear, burst through the hotel room door with
their double-barrelled twelve-gauge shotguns. Shepard's peculiar blend of nostalgia mixed with more than a touch of parody
is perhaps best summed up in the words of the title character
to Sluefoot Sue in *The Sad Lament of Pecos Bill on the Eve of Killing His Wife*: "Why is we forsaken/ Lost and shamed, forgotten/
Why is we both rotten/ In the memories of man."[23]

Shepard's first naturalistic dramatization of the conflict between the claims of the past and the realities of the present
occurs in *True West* when Lee, the natural man, the wanderer,
the adventurer, arrives to challenge his brother Austin, the pale
quasi-intellectual suburbanite. On the surface, *True West* seems
but one more addition to the woefully overworked tradition of
the American psychological family drama. But what begins as

comic sibling rivalry gradually builds until hilarity becomes
hysteria as myth collides with reality in a dramatic clash of cultural abstractions.

In a neatly-ordered pristine kitchen and adjoining alcove of
a southern California suburb, Austin works by candlelight on
his screenplay as *True West* opens. Taking advantage of the solitude and absence from his wife and children while house-
sitting for his vacationing mother, he practices his art. His concentration is broken by the unexpected and unwelcome arrival
of his older brother Lee, a "desert rat" who returns hostile and
deranged from a long sojourn on the Mojave desert. Suffused
in moonlight, Lee seems a patently unreal, almost hallucinatory character. Shockingly out of place in Mom and Austin's
organized world, Lee's words and gestures emanate violence
and chaos. When he announces that he neither eats nor sleeps,
his words seem somehow threatening. Lee belongs to a lost
frontier and the wild perils of the old West; the tidy set that
cannot contain him contributes to his alien quality.

The two brothers have nothing in common but mutual hostility, born primarily of envy. Austin secretly longs for Lee's
freedom and independence; Lee openly desires Austin's comfort and security. But Austin is determined that through "civilized" behavior and facile cordiality he can keep the repressed
anger in check. He feels, at once, fear of and pity for his brother.
Lee is not so deranged that he fails to intuit the smug intellectual superiority of his brother, and, is bent on releasing the hidden truths that lie behind social behavior. Lee bombards the
appearance of an amiable order that Austin attempts to con-
struct. His verbal and physical assaults result in exposing the
limits of Austin's psychological endurance.

Despite Austin's efforts to maintain an atmosphere of filial
affection, Lee insidiously breaks through his defenses and establishes a conflict by exposing his brother's hidden desires and
motives. He begins by calling attention to the symbolic attributes of the candle that illuminates Austin's writing table: "You
always work by candlelight? . . . Isn't that what the old guys
did? The Forefathers? Candlelight burning into the night?"[24]
Austin resists the analogy and its romantic implications. The
association between his creative efforts and emblems from the

past makes Austin uneasy; in fact, Austin is uncomfortable with any reference to his art. He deprecatingly refers to the "simple romance" that he is writing as "just a little research" (p. 6).

Lee misinterprets Austin's insecurity about his work and imagines that his brother is playing down his accomplishment to spare his feelings since Lee is clearly not the artistic type. But Lee protests that he once "fooled around" with art himself but gave it up for more practical endeavors. Then he adds defensively, "It was ahead of its time" (p. 6). Sensing the potential danger in pursuing this dialogue, Austin changes the subject to the "old man," their father whose life has been ruined by heavy drinking and who lives on the desert estranged from his family. This conversation proves to be even more explosive because of the affinity between Lee's behavior and his father's. Recognizing that each verbal path he pursues leads to an impasse, Austin subtly expresses concern about the purpose and duration of Lee's visit. When Lee announces his intention to case the neighborhood, following his vocation of stealing and pawning small household appliances, Austin refuses to loan him his car for such a purpose and offers him money instead. The gesture enrages Lee, who lunges at Austin and begins shaking him violently, accusing Austin of treating him like the "old man" whom he bought off with "Hollywood blood money" (p. 8).

The sibling rivalry is exaggerated to murderous proportions as Lee brutally plunges into the truth of the brothers' relationship. In sharp contrast to Austin's artificial cordiality, Lee insists upon stripping away all pretense. Unlike his brother, Lee does not traffic in fiction and makes only the slightest effort to conceal or control his aggression. When Austin denies him the use of the car, Lee cajoles his brother for a few moments with promises to take good care of the car and return it safely; but when this tact fails, he quickly asserts: "Then I'll just take the damn thing" (p. 8), viciously reminding Austin that the social game they are playing thinly conceals a virulent aggression. Lee's primitive force and native intuition is thus pitted against Austin's refined manners and acquired wit, a conflict that transcends the psychic rivalry of the two individualized characters and opens Shepard's play to an allegorical reading. The battle between force and wit or primitive power and acquired learning develops further into an exploration of the nature of human creativity when Lee usurps Austin's role as a screenwriter. At the end of scene 2 as Austin anticipates a meeting with Saul Kimmer, the producer who is interested in his script, Lee says that he has a couple "projects" Kimmer might be interested in. The preposterous story that Lee offers Kimmer has all the credibility of a contemporary scandal sheet. But in an hilarious comment on the state of commercialism in the arts, especially in the film industry which is a particular concern of Shepard's, Kimmer accepts Lee's project based on its verisimilitude, rejects Austin's simple romance, and insists that Austin edit his brother's work.

As the lights dim slowly at the end of Act I, Lee dictates the narrative of his screenplay as Austin types:

"So they take off after each other straight into an endless black prairie. The sun is just comin' down and they can feel the night on their backs. What they don't know is that each one of 'em is afraid, see. Each one separately thinks that he's the only one that's afraid. And they keep ridin' like that straight into the night. Not knowing. And the one who's chasin' doesn't know where the other one is taking him. And the one who's being chased doesn't know where he's going." (p. 27)

In the Magic Theatre's premiere production of *True West*, the actors in this scene exchanged fearful, suspicious glances, then quickly looked away. The implications were clear: Lee's narrative is, ironically, "true-to-life," but as a fictive correlative of the brothers' dramatic conflict. Like the cowboys in Lee's western chase scene, Lee and Austin are locked in an endless pursuit.

Shepard thus establishes a powerful dialectic between the truth of fiction and the falsity of life. Although Austin is the writer in the family, it is Lee, ironically, who will convince Saul Kimmer that his screenplay is "true-to-life." And it is Lee who really is in touch with the harsher realities of human behavior. Austin believes that because they are brothers they are incapable of inflicting violence upon one another. Lee scoffs at his brother's naiveté, reminding him that family members are precisely the people who engage in physical violence with the most frequency. Brothers are at the top of Lee's list. As a writer with "an ivy-league diploma," Austin should be aware of the truth in his brother's statement. A bond of blood did not prevent Cain from killing Abel; Austin and Lee are equally susceptible to a primordial battle despite the centuries of "civilization" that have intervened since that first murder. Lee and Austin are motivated by envy, but their actions are held in check by fear. For each brother sees in the other a potential self that lurks within his own psychology, but both are afraid of being overtaken by this unrealized part of their character that could destroy the image that they presently hold of themselves.

In Act II the brothers continue to argue about truth and fiction and the authenticity of their respective professions. An incredulous Austin grapples with Kimmer's decision to accept Lee's screenplay. Kimmer insists that Lee's story is true because Lee "is speaking from experience" (p. 35). But Austin protests that his way of life is the authentic one:

"I drive on the freeway every day. I swallow the smog. I watch the news in color. I shop in the Safeway. I'm the one who's in touch. Not him!" (p. 35)

But Kimmer ignores Austin's argument and continues to negotiate with Lee. Secure in the role he has appropriated from his brother, Lee calmly assumes his new position. Austin's only recourse is to adopt Lee's former station in life. In the brilliantly comic stage picture that opens scene 7, the reversal of roles is presented. It is nightfall again as it was in scene 1, but now it is Lee who sits hunched over the typewriter working by candlelight while Austin lies sprawled drunkenly on the floor. Austin's rendition of "Red Sails in the Sunset" infuriates Lee, who is trying to concentrate. Conscious of the ironic reversal of roles, Austin taunts Lee, "Now I'm the intruder" (p. 38). While Lee struggles to write his script, Austin vows to earn his living by making a little tour of the neighborhood and stealing some toasters as Lee earlier had stolen televisions. But before he leaves to conquer Lee's territory since his brother has usurped his own, Austin tells Lee a story about their father, a vividly detailed narrative that is both comic and pathetic about the old man's tortured trek to the border to be fitted with a pair of false teeth by a Mexican dentist. Austin relates his attempt to do something nice for his father by taking him out to dinner at a Chinese restaurant. But the old man only wanted to drink and took his new teeth out, placing them in the doggie bag with the chop suey that he left on the bar. "Now that's a true story. True to life" (p. 42), Austin tells Lee as the scene ends. Austin then has his own true-to-life story to challenge Lee's screenplay, and in the process of telling the tale Austin is finally able to express the anger and resentment he feels toward his father. The loss of teeth symbolizes the father's impotence; Austin's impulse to recount the story occurs significantly at the moment when he feels his own impotence keenly and when he has developed into a mirror image of his elder brother, the father's surrogate. The brothers are equally incapable of communicating their hidden fears and desires in life; but in the fictions they create, the truth of their inner experiences surfaces.

Austin and Lee not only have exchanged occupations but have also created characters of themselves modeled on each other's personalities. Neither one of them, however, is complete without the other. Lee confesses that he needs Austin's help in delineating the fictional characters in his play, and Austin will soon plead for Lee's assistance in helping him escape from his artificial world. When scene 8 opens Austin appears to have successfully carried out the demands of Lee's trade, but Lee has clearly failed to adjust to his new profession.

Lee smashes the typewriter with a golf club and burns his manuscript as Austin proudly displays the loot from his overnight adventure—a dozen shiny chrome toasters lined up on the kitchen counter. Austin's success has aroused in him a desire to pursue Lee's way of life and to leave behind what he now perceives as his superficial existence. What were once important and meaningful landmarks in his hometown now strike Austin as unfamiliar and false . . . "replicas of streets I remember. Streets I can't tell if I lived on or saw in a postcard" (p. 49). Lee's frustrated attempt to assimilate into Austin's culture has led him to recognize his own unsuitability for urban life. Both brothers now possess the same goal. Austin implores

Lee to take him to live on the desert despite the latter's insistence that his way of life was not "some kinda philosophical decision" but a result of his inability to "make it in the city" (p. 49).

Austin remains adamant in his decision and by the end of the scene the brothers have effected a deal. Austin will write Lee's screenplay, giving him full credit for the work; Lee, in return, will take Austin to live on the desert. Austin seems to have controlled, temporarily, Lee's hostility, but the scene pulsates with an undercurrent of violence that soon erupts with great force. The agreed–upon collaboration is ritually sealed when Lee takes a slow, deliberate bite from the toast that Austin has referred to as the symbol of a new beginning, "like salvation sort of" (p. 48).

The following scene presents Austin desperately trying to fulfill his part of the bargain as he suffers Lee's violent explosions, which accompany the dictation of his screenplay. The brothers' role reversal could have led to a resolution of their conflict, but instead of understanding and sympathy, the transference of roles has produced a more intense desperation. The stage emblems convey the aftermath of turbulent battle: the beer cans littering the floor, the smashed typewriter, the dead plants, the telephone ripped out of the wall, the crumbled toast and battered toasters. The lighting is intense yellow, an effect Shepard describes in a stage direction "like a desert junkyard at high noon" (p. 50). The stage is thus set for the final showdown between the two brothers.

Into this ravaged scene walks Lee and Austin's mother, home early from her vacation in Alaska. Mom immediately begins to remind her sons of their former roles and fundamental differences. She cannot accept her sons' new relationship and expresses dismay when Austin tells her that Lee has sold a screenplay. "Lee did? Not you?" (p. 53) she questions Austin. She also voices her disapproval of Austin's plan to accompany Lee to the desert, insisting that her younger son could not survive under such conditions.

Mom's unexpected return causes Lee to abandon immediately the covenant he had made with Austin. Jolted back into reality, Lee resolves to return to his wilderness home and rejects Austin's pleas to accompany him. His experience with his brother, however, has left some impression on Lee, for he insists on taking his mother's antique china and silverware with him into the desert. Lee may simply follow his old habits and pawn the merchandise, but he claims: "I'm tired of eatin' outa' my bare hands, ya' know. It's not civilized" (p. 56). Nevertheless, Lee openly renounces the life represented by his mother and brother that he had once coveted. As he readies to leave he announces his intention never to return to a town that could "drive a man insane" as it has his brother (p. 57). Lee has come to appreciate the values of his own perilous and insecure freedom by witnessing Austin's transformation into a man of passion and aggression who desperately needs the way of life he imagines he will find on the desert. Austin's vision of existence on the desert may well be a fabrication of romantic notions of noble savagery and harmony with nature. He is, after all, a writer of romantic fiction. But Lee recognizes the potential for insanity that Austin's "civilization" breeds; thus, he chooses to revert to his former way of life, this time having made a conscious decision based on his experience.

Austin, however, does not abandon his new dream. He has firmly resolved to reject the life of the artist, which he now views as artificial, for the authenticity he believes life on the desert will afford. "There's nothin' real down here," he tells Lee, "Least of all me!" (p. 49). Austin's resolution is reinforced by his mother's comical confusion regarding an advertisement about a local Picasso exhibit. She excitedly reports to her sons that Picasso is in town, and insists that all three of them go to the local museum to meet the great artist. As we would expect, Lee has never heard of Picasso, but Austin tries to explain that Picasso is dead. Mom has, of course, confused the artist's life with his work; and thus in this comic dialogue between the mother and her sons, Shepard again introduces the difficulty in discerning life from art, an ongoing dialectic in the play that has been a constant source of discussion and contention as Austin tries to convince Lee that his "true-to-life" screenplay is unnatural and false. Now, however, Austin denies that Lee's story is "dumb" (i.e. unrealistic) and insists that it has a validity that transcends the account of "two lamebrains chasin' each

other across Texas" (p. 56). Mom, a patently plastic version of
the values that Austin had once endorsed as genuine, has in
her ignorance strengthened Austin's realization that what he
had once viewed as art was only artifice.

William Kleb has elaborated on the role reversal in *True West*
by suggesting that it is a metaphorical representation of "the
divided self," a familiar condition in modern drama. Shepard's
innovative presentation of the divided self, according to Kleb,
consists in taking an "imprint" of R. D. Laing's state of "primary ontological insecurity," rather than simply describing the
state of mind as Beckett and Pinter have done before Shepard.[25] Kleb quotes Laing's assertion that in the divided self
"there is a rent in his relation with himself; he does not experience himself as a complete person but rather a split in various
ways."[26] Kleb argues for *True West* as Shepard's "most subjective, most personal play to date"[27] by calling attention to well-
known facts of the author's biography: his childhood on a small
farm in southern California; his literary and film successes that
link Shepard with Austin; and his self-dramatization as a "cowboy," not unlike Lee. Finally the fact that Shepard has *no* brother
convinces Kleb that *True West* is an enactment of the playwright's personal conflict. In other words, Kleb sees Austin and
Lee as two halves of Shepard's character. More recently, Tucker
Orbison has delineated the brothers' conflict in Jungian terms,
Lee representing the shadow figure "as emotional, autonomous, and possessive." In these psychoanalytic terms, the play
dramatizes a "confrontation between the conscious ego (Austin) and the hidden psychic forces (Lee)."[28]

Without question Shepard is a highly self-conscious playwright whose dramatic characters and the conflicts they enact
are drawn from his own imaginative experience. And, in fact,
Lee and Austin are, to some extent, comically exaggerated as-
pects of the author's personality. More importantly, Shepard
depicts Austin and Lee as cultural archetypes drawn on the
outer edges of realism. That they do represent two halves of a
character that Shepard strives to integrate seems much more
important than autobiographical speculation; for it is in the attempt to bring the two opposites into concert that Shepard's

concept of the "true west" is explored, and it is in the failed integration that the play approaches tragedy.

The true west of the title is more than a pun on the defunct western magazine of the same name. The American West for Shepard has always represented freedom and authenticity in previous plays. The West also is suggestive of psychological introspection. In *Angel City* (1976), Rabbit Brown, the voodoo magician/dreamer, carries a medicine bundle that holds the secret of the four points on the compass and emblems that depict their respective position. The West he designates, "the Looks-Within-Place," a place of introspective discovery and a kind of Pandora's box that will release a terrible force upon the world if its contents are ever explored. For Rabbit, the West is the only authentic bundle; the other three points on the compass are imitations. In *True West*, the West is both a geographical reality and a psychological frontier; and it is on this psychic frontier that the battle between Austin and Lee takes place.

In Henry Nash Smith's *Virgin Land: The American West as Symbol and Myth*, the author repeatedly refers to Frederick Jackson Turner's seminal treatise, "The Significance of the Frontier in American History." Smith cites Turner's "most important debt to his intellectual tradition . . . the ideas of savagery and civilization that he uses to define his central factor, the frontier. His [Turner's] frontier is the *meeting point* between savagery and civilization" (emphasis mine).[29] The metaphorical extension of Turner's frontier concept is clearly played out in *True West* when the savage Lee meets the civilized Austin. In Smith's discussion of the mythic resonance of "The Great American Desert," he quotes Washington Irving's description of the inhabitants of this unsettled wilderness as

mongrel races . . . the remains of broken and almost extinguished tribes, the descendants of hunters and trappers; of fugitives from the Spanish and American frontiers; of adventurers and desperadoes of every class and country yearly ejected from the bosom of society into the wilderness.[30]

Such a character is Shepard's Lee, nomadic and predatory, emerging mysteriously from the desert where he has lived for an undetermined time and in inconceivable circumstances. Lee brings with him into his mother's suburban home only the values of self-preservation and an innate primitivism that cannot be subdued by all of Austin's efforts to tame his brother's wildness and placate his desperation. Austin, the antithesis of his brother, depends for his survival on all the institutions of society that support individuals who are physically weak but learn to survive by their wit. Without the freeways and the Safeways, Austin would become easy prey to man's baser instincts.

In the clash between these two opposites and the futile effort to integrate the two, *True West* approaches tragedy. Turner's geographical meeting place between savagery and civilization is extended by Shepard into a psychological boundary. And it is on this precipitous edge, the frontier that defines the limits of their experience, that Lee and Austin struggle against a cultural determinism which they represent as allegorical figures in the clash between East and West. But on another level, Lee and Austin strive to overcome the character traits and values inherited from their parents, for their division and conflict are equally due to Lee's close association with his father and Austin's with his mother.

Robert Corrigan has described the essence of the tragic spirit with an extended metaphor that is particularly apposite for Austin's fate:

in the tragic situation man finds himself in a primitive country that he had believed his forefathers had tamed, civilized, and charted, only to discover they had not. One of the greatest holds that tragedy has always had on the imagination is that it brings us into direct touch with the naked landscape.[31]

Lee is the visible manifestation of that primitive country, the instinct for aggression and the power of intuition that Austin has denied. The "naked landscape" that Austin finally confronts is his own need to return to a world closer to the natural primitivism of his brother and the potential for such action that lies within him.

Furthermore, the conflict in Shepard's play conforms pre-

cisely to Corrigan's insistence on the "inner dividedness" of
the tragic protagonist that causes all "significant catastrophic
events."[32] Shepard's brothers are, in fact, doubly divided. First,
they are, in one sense, two halves of the same character; thus,
in two characters Shepard manifests the divided self described
by Kleb. Saul Kimmer, the producer in the play, thinks that
Lee and Austin are the same person, and Kleb points out that
metaphorically they are.[33] But Austin and Lee are also suffi-
ciently individualized to be divided within each of their autonomous personalities. The confrontation with the other awakens
that part of their character that has been dormant or repressed
and that cannot coexist with their chosen self-images. The conflict in the play thus occurs both *between* the two brothers (the
geographical or cultural frontier) and *within* each of the individual characters (the psychological boundary).

Lee's battle remains primarily an external one with his brother,
but Austin finds himself face to face with his own instinctive
aggression, which he has tried to deny. Austin, then, fulfills
the threatened violence that has hovered over the play's action
since Lee's arrival. Wrapping a telephone cord around his
brother's throat and forcing him to the floor, Austin intends to
compel Lee to stay. But his sudden, impulsive violence leads
Austin to an impasse and obliges him to see the futility of
aggression. He cannot expect to control Lee by constantly
threatening to murder him, nor can he achieve his goal by killing Lee. But now, if he releases his stranglehold, he faces Lee's
certain retaliation. Faced with this dilemma, Austin vows to
live on the desert alone, recognizing perhaps that his action
has made him unfit for the society of other people. Lee continues to lie motionless on the floor, and for a moment it appears
that Austin has killed his brother. But as Austin runs toward
the door, Lee agilely springs forward to bar his brother's exit.
Shepard describes the final impression of his play as the stage
gradually darkens:

the figures of the brothers now appear to be caught in a vast desert-
like landscape, they are very still but watchful for the next move, lights
go slowly to black as the after–image of the brothers pulses in the
dark. (p. 60)

One critic has described this compelling image as "the mystical death embrace of two fratricidal brothers."[34] But still, it is the father, even though he is physically absent, whose shadow the brothers grapple with. Austin faces him first in combat with his brother, the very image of the old man, then within himself, as he becomes a mirror image of the patriarchal qualities he tried to repress. As both men face each other, crouched and ready to renew the battle, *True West* ends in a frightful vision of unresolved, eternal conflict.

In Shepard's first three naturalistic plays, the father appears prominently as a figure that the sons strive to excise. In *Curse of the Starving Class* Wesley becomes transformed into his father Weston by adopting his gestures, assuming his habits, and wearing his clothes. At the end of the play it is not clear whether Wesley is free of his father's infectious influence or carries forward the curse of the father, the poisonous genetic inheritance. In *Buried Child* Vince's journey toward self-discovery takes him into the past, where he encounters Dodge. When Vince's behavior indicates that he has psychologically inherited his grandfather's character, Dodge acknowledges Vince as his true son and heir. Lee and Austin in *True West* live with a constant concern for and anxiety about "the old man." Both brothers disassociate themselves from their father, whose degeneration frightens and repulses them. Austin's story about his father's loss of teeth symbolically suggests sexual impotence; the story itself may represent the son's wish fulfillment. But in reality Austin and Lee cannot escape from their father's influence. These three plays leave the father and son conflicts unresolved.

FOOL FOR LOVE

In Shepard's next play, *Fool for Love* (1983), the father becomes the focus of attention as a powerful attempt is made to expel him from the lives of the characters. In this play Shepard returns to the use of an obvious anti–illusionistic device. Not only does the father disturb the harmony of his progenies' lives, but he also represents a threat to the play's dramatic illusion as he sits in his rocking chair swigging Jim Beam outside the frame of the proscenium. The father in *Fool for Love* is the in-

carnation of the old man in *True West* whom we never see. As
an interesting digression, he is also an almost exact likeness of
Shepard's real father. A photograph of Shepard's father in *Motel Chronicles* confirms the uncanny resemblance to the actor who
played the father in *Fool for Love* at New York's Circle Repertory Theatre, a production that Shepard directed himself. Further similarities between the playwright's dramatic fathers and
his actual father are borne out by this excerpt from *Motel
Chronicles*:

My Dad has a collection of cigarette butts in a Yuban coffee can. I
bought him a carton of Old Golds but he wouldn't touch them. He
sneered at my carton of Cigarettes, all red and white and ready-rolled.
He spent all the food money I'd gave [sic] him on Bourbon. Filled the
ice box with bottles. Had his hair cut short like a WWII fighter pilot.
He gleamed everytime he ran his hand across the bristles. Said they
used to cut it short like that so their helmets would fit. Showed me
how the shrapnel scars still showed on the nape of his neck. . . . My
Dad lives alone on the desert. He says he doesn't fit with people.

4/79

Santa Fe, New Mexico[35]

The action of Shepard's quartet of domestic dramas may be
purely imaginative, but the father figure is clearly modeled on
Shepard's own. Biographical speculations aside, *Fool for Love*
moves toward a resolution of the conflict that has been a large
part of Shepard's drama since 1976; the play also indicates a
return to earlier dramatic techniques. Pete Hamill points out
that in the later plays . . . "the symbol of the circle recurs. The
characters are imprisoned within the circle of their lives, or seem
to be making a wide circle home, as does Shepard himself."[36]
Thinking perhaps of Edward Albee's *The Zoo Story*, one of the
first plays he remembers seeing in New York, Shepard says:
"It's like you gotta go a long way away to come back. . . .
Something like that."[37] The line that Shepard tries to remember may be Jerry's in Albee's play: "Sometime it's necessary to
go a long distance out of the way in order to come back a short
distance correctly."[38] Jerry makes this statement when he realizes that the love/hate relationship he once had was prefera-
ble to the indifference he now must live with. Shepard's char-

acters find a similar truth in the wide circle home of *Fool for Love*, but first they must confront the father who controls their lives and manipulates Shepard's play.

As *Fool for Love* opens, May sits inertly on a shabby motel-room bed without responding to Eddie's efforts to draw her into action or conversation. When he offers to leave, the frozen image of dejection comes to life with sudden fury as May lashes out at her lover. The opening moments represent a lull in a violent lovers' quarrel that appears to have been going on for many years. Eddie, we learn, has traced May to a run-down motel on the edge of the Mojave desert, where she has gone to begin a new life, ending their fifteen-year-old relationship because of his repeated infidelities. Having grown tired of his latest consort, an enigmatic "Countess," Eddie has driven over two thousand miles to offer May the time-worn excuse that the Countess means nothing to him and that May is his real love. May alternates wildly between demanding that Eddie leave and begging him to stay. She arouses his jealousy by dressing seductively for a date scheduled for that evening. The argument grows more violent.

Shepard's characters in this play are highly stereotypical. May is the woman who cannot live with her man or without him; Eddie is an insensitive "love 'em and leave 'em" cowboy, complete with shotgun and lasso. The father sits silently observing the action from his rocking chair for a long time, but then begins to speak, commenting on the action first as a spectator and then editing and correcting May's and Eddie's words and actions as if he were the author. The space that the father occupies, together with his commentary, suggests that he is a substitute for the author or director (in this case they are one and the same). A similar technique has been used in some productions of Pirandello's *Six Characters in Search of an Author* when an empty chair has been placed just outside of the frame evoking the willfully absent but omnipresent author whose absence has relegated his characters to types, frozen in the moment of crisis, struggling to free themselves from the confines of art and escape into life.

But the chair in *Fool for Love* is occupied, and the old man is more realistically the author of the painful and desperate scene

that Eddie and May seem fated to play again and again. Although he claims not to recognize the two characters, the old
man is unquestionably the father of both of them and is re-
sponsible for the tortured affair that Eddie and May are unable
to relinquish. Eddie recognizes his father's presence and exchanges nods of complicity with him, but the two men only
speak to each other when May is absent. In the first father and
son interchange, the old man tells Eddie to look at a picture on
the wall (the walls are bare), and asks him if he knows the
woman in the picture. Although Eddie clearly sees nothing, he
plays along with his father and even manages to suppress his
disbelief when his father tells him that the woman in the picture is Barbara Mandrell and she is his wife. "That's realism,"
he tells his son. "Can you understand that?"[39] Eddie obviously
does not understand but he nods affirmatively and the old man
expresses his pleasure in the understanding that they have
reached. The father's admission that he is "actually married to
Barbara Mandrell in [his] mind" causes an audience to wonder
how much of the onstage action also occurs in the mind of this
irresponsible author.

The relationship between Eddie and May, their psychological
confusion, and the ensuing violent arguments seem to be the
result of the past action of the father. May and Eddie's brutal
dispute reveals that their father led two different lives with two
wives in separate towns and had one child with each of them.
He would disappear for months at a time and each wife would
gratefully receive him upon his return without questioning his
absence. Finally, however, May's mother decided to trace her
wandering husband and found him in the small town where
he lived with Eddie's mother, who committed suicide when
she learned the truth. At least, this is the way May tells the
story. In Eddie's version, his father silently led him on a long
walk to the door of the house where May lived with her mother.
Eddie saw his half-sister May peering from behind the dress of
the red-haired woman who opened the door and threw herself
sobbing into the arms of her long absent husband. Instantly
they fell in love, still unaware of the truth of their heritage.

The father further confuses the facts by denying both stories
and insinuating that he might not have fathered both children.

But incest is not really the issue in *Fool for Love*. It is alluded to
in Eddie's references to a mysterious bond between himself and
May which he mentions when on the verge of losing control of
her altogether. Her reaction of horror and vicious reminder that
this bond must remain unspoken hints at its forbidden nature.
But much more important is the psychological inheritance from
father to son and mother to daughter. Eddie, like his father, is
unable to remain faithful to one woman and yearns for the ex-
citement of a life elevated above everyday, mundane reality.
His attachment to the Countess, who is never seen and perhaps does not really exist, is evidence of this desire. Further
likenesses are reinforced by the camaraderie they share over
the bottle of whiskey that is passed from father to son and is
significantly the only action that demands a physical crossing
of the boundary between the play and the frame. May obviously resembles her mother in her dependence upon a man
whom she cannot trust and who treats her badly. The action
of the play consists in the young couple's attempt to escape
from the psychological patterns imposed upon them by their
parents and their effort to solve the dilemma of the relationship
created by their father's hypocrisy.

We learn that over the past fifteen years Eddie and May have
been separated and reunited many times, each time playing
out this same scene of violence and confusion. Their lives and
their love have been patterned as a circle of cruelty and deceit.
In the play, for the first time, the characters painfully recall the
details of their past as they honestly remember them. As they
search for the truth that will end this cycle of treachery, the
father must be banished from intrusion into his children's lives.
Shepard's play does not suggest that an absolute truth can be
discovered, for Eddie and May can never agree upon a defini-
tive version of their past.

There is a tentative promise of compromise and acceptance
as the lovers slowly join in an embrace that blocks the father
from their consciousness. When the old man leaves his rocking
chair and encircles the embracing couple, demanding that they
play the scene according to his idea of truth, the young couple
no longer acknowledge his dictates or even his presence. The
illusion created by the father seems to vanish as the lovers unite,

seizing their lives from the scenario authored by the past. Eddie momentarily ignores his father's ruthless call to join forces
with him against their common enemy, the woman. But the
son's triumph is transient; for although he refuses to acknowledge his father's presence, he cannot silence the promptings of
an inner voice, an unconscious pull, that leads him away from
the reality of May's love and out into the desert, that illusory,
eminently male landscape that summons Shepard's heroes with
a siren more seductive than Circe. Like the other plays in the
domestic quartet, *Fool for Love* ends with an action that emphasizes the ineluctable power of inherited mental structures. None
of Shepard's heroes transcend the destructive influence of the
father. Together, these four plays are a succession of tones on
a tragic scale.

Commenting on *True West* Shepard has said: "I think we're
split in a much more devastating way than psychology can ever
reveal. It's not so cute. Not some little thing we can get over.
It's something we've got to live with."[40] If Lee and Austin are
images of this profound division captured in eternal conflict,
May and Eddie in *Fool for Love* are fully realized and sympa-
thetic survivors of this profound division between lovers who
are, at least, half conscious of the split, but incapable of resolv-
ing it.

A LIE OF THE MIND

Of all of Shepard's characters, Beth and Jake in *A Lie of the
Mind* (1985) are the most profoundly shattered victims of gender conflict and nuclear family psychology. In this play Shepard expands his cast of characters to include two families as
he continues to explore all facets of the domestic battles he has
been staging for the past decade.

As *A Lie of the Mind* opens, Jake chokes out a crazed confes-
sion of murdering his wife, Beth, to Frankie who listens with
mounting horror. Jake and Frankie resemble the split–self
brothers Lee and Austin in *True West*, the former filled with
brutal anger and violence, the latter open to sensitive discussion and reasoned compromise. Jake is a close cousin to Eddie
in *Fool for Love*. Minus the cowboy gear, Jake resembles Shep-

ard's former protagonist in his demented capacity for love.
Together with Shepard's screenplay, hero Travis in *Paris, Texas*,
Jake and Eddie form a threesome of heroes who cannot separate love from possessive desire. In *A Lie of the Mind* Shepard
concentrates on the causes and effects of domestic violence.
The immediate result of Jake's unchecked assault on his wife is
presented with shocking effect in the second scene as the play
shifts to Beth's hospital room where she struggles to compre-
hend what has happened to her. Left for dead by Jake, Beth
was rescued by her brother, Mike, who found her badly brain-
damaged, her speech seriously inhibited, her motor skills badly
impaired, and her thought processes confused and dramati-
cally limited.

The rest of the cast includes Jake's sister Sally and mother
Lorraine; and Beth's father Baylor and mother Meg. Shepard
uses the simple convention of alternating scenes from family to
family, juxtaposing one with the other with only the music of
a country and western band, the Red Clay Ramblers, to provide transitions. His point is as clear as it was in the quartet of
family plays that precedes *A Lie of the Mind*: the curse of psychological disease passes from parents to children; the family's buried secrets eventually surface to demand confrontation; the truth of our experience collides with the lies of our
minds.

Shepard works his obsessive theme of the truth in art versus
reality into this play as well. While there are many lies of the
mind in this play, the one that functions as an immediate cause
is Jake's conviction that his wife is having an affair. His jealousy is instigated by Beth's role in a play in which she acts as
a seductress. As a method actor she practices becoming the
character, and her rehearsals enter her personal life as she en-
lists her husband to read the lines of her leading man. Jake's
suspicions multiply as he watches his wife transform herself.
In particular he becomes obsessed with the ritualistic oiling of
her body, an action she performs with growing regularity in
preparation for performances. He interprets her lack of sexual
interest as a sign of infidelity since he is unable to conceive of
a woman whose career becomes self-absorbing. When she refuses to relinquish her role in the play, he assaults her.

In one rare moment, both sides of the stage are illuminated

as Jake stands on the left holding the box that contains his father's ashes; on the other side Beth enters slowly in a low-cut satin gown, sits down on a satin-draped sofa, and begins to rub oil into her breasts and shoulders. This silent juxtaposition connects Jake's unresolved grief for his father with the illusion he holds about his wife. When we meet Lorraine, Jake's suffocating and domineering mother, it becomes clear that Jake's oedipal dilemma is still a very active part of his mental life. His transference of love-object from mother to wife is a process that Lorraine chooses to deny (she can't even remember Beth's name). Jake's intense fear of abandonment leads to physical violence when he is threatened with the loss of his love-object. Ironically Beth continues to long for her abusive husband even as she lies in the hospital painfully attempting to regain her speech. With her verbal capacity severely limited, Beth's childlike sentences, torturously executed, reverberate with complex truth about the urgent dependency and desperation of lovers' relationships. If I never see him again, she says, "then I be dead."[41]

As in the other domestic dramas, Shepard suggests that the problem lies within the minds of his male protagonists. The fact that Beth is a woman without a sense of self outside of her relationship with a man is a problem that Shepard does not directly address. From a profoundly male perspective, Shepard instead focuses again on father/son relationships, leaving his women characters to clean up the debris. The immediate action of *A Lie of the Mind* is contained squarely within the arena of gender conflict; but the origin of the conflict is in the father's relationship with his son.

The fathers in Shepard's plays are consistently cruel, violent, manipulative, and demented. In *A Lie of the Mind* Beth's father, Baylor, is detached from the family, absorbed in his favorite pastime, hunting, a sport that allows him to redirect his power-hungry and bloodthirsty passion away from his family, rendering him a relatively innocuous pale shadow of Shepard's former fathers. Jake's father is dead. The American flag that draped his coffin lies folded under his son's bed alongside the box that contains his ashes. According to sister Sally, Jake accomplished what Shepard's other dramatic sons attempted or dreamed of—killing their father. In a variation on Austin's story in *True West*

about bar-hopping with his alcoholic father in Mexico, Sally tells
her mother that she watched helplessly while Jake dared his
drunken father to race him to the American border, stopping
at every bar on the way. The son easily outdistanced his father
who ran in front of a truck on the highway and was killed
while Jake sat quietly drinking in a bar several miles up the
road. Sally insists that Jake killed their father while Lorraine
hysterically protests that her son is incapable of such a violent
act. But as she witnesses her son becoming more and more like
her husband, whom she both despises and adores, Lorraine
cries out in desperation: "The circle has to have an end, a snake
can't bite his tail forever."[42] Lorraine is finally left alone with
Sally, a daughter who has really never known her mother's
love. Together they conclude that all men are hopeless as they
burn down the house with all their possessions and leave for
Ireland to look up long–lost relatives.

Meanwhile, at their former neighbors' home, Meg is reach-
ing a similar conclusion. A woman deadened by the absence of
real feeling in her life, Meg slavishly attends her husband and
children and accepts the emptiness of her existence in exchange for a quiet and orderly home. The superficial harmony
of her life becomes hysterically distorted when her husband
shoots Frankie in the leg, mistaking him for a deer, and brings
him home for the women to nurse. With Frankie a wounded
prisoner in her home, her daughter unmanageably disturbed,
and her husband callously indifferent, Meg begins to question
some basic assumptions about nuclear family dynamics. With
childlike insight Meg comes up with a basic theory: "the female
needs the other, the male, but the male doesn't need the other,
the female, in the same way. . . . He doesn't know what he
needs; so he goes off to be alone, and dies alone."[43] With this
recognition she recommends that Baylor leave since "all these
women" are such a burden to him. She refuses to wait on him
anymore, leaving him immobilized in his easy chair with a bad
back. She tosses his socks into his lap, but he is unable to put
them on his freezing feet.

The stage images in A Lie of the Mind come close to the absurdist tableaux of an Ionesco play. In a post-absurdist parody
like Tom Stoppard's After Magritte, the inchoate opening is ra-

tionally explicated in the dialogue that follows. The action of Shepard's play comically exaggerates the existence of his characters in situations that approach the dark comedy of absurdism or post-absurdism. At the same time, however, he poses serious questions that call for psychological resolution in a realistic vein.

Violence as a necessary ingredient for passionate love on the part of American men is portrayed as a lamentable truth. Perhaps we are meant to see some hope for emotional and sexual love between men and women in Frankie and Beth's final embrace (one that remains unbroken unlike Eddie and May's aborted reconciliation in *Fool for Love*). But Beth doesn't even know who Frankie is; she accepts him as a desperate replacement for Jake. And Frankie seems to accept Beth as a gift from his brother, who sanctions their union. At the play's end Beth and her mother Meg are lost in romantic ideology about the "real wedding" that they anticipate. Although the characters' pathology is singularly contemporary, the genre is reminiscent of Restoration comedy, with its wildly farcical treatment of family and gender politics. And as in the case of Restoration comedy, Shepard has created a host of types: the violently love-starved hero who can only answer love with power and domination (Lee, Eddie, Travis, Jake); the submissive, vulnerable heroine who sacrifices herself for romantic ideology (May, Beth); the suffocating, possessive mother (Halie, Mom in *True West*, Lorraine); the brutal controlling patriarch (Dodge, Weston, *True West*'s and *Fool for Love*'s "old men," Baylor and the dead father in *A Lie of the Mind*). In this, the longest of Shepard's family plays, there is a longing for a resolution to some of the questions it engenders, but that resolution never comes.

In five plays Shepard turns his crystal of common themes, illuminating each facet time and again, always returning to the same basic problems. The death of Shepard's father in 1983 left him "with a yearning for some kind of resolution which could never be."[44]

On the evening that *A Lie of the Mind* previewed, Shepard worked intently on the script as he watched the production. Perhaps he will seek a way to resolve some of the urgency in this play's action, or even answer a few of the questions it poses.

Aesthetically, the play could have ended a number of times before its formal closure—any one of them would have been as satisfying theoretically as the moment when the play did end. There is a terrible grappling here and an unabated anxiousness that avoids psychological resolve, but makes for powerful drama.

Since its modest beginnings at Theatre Genesis, Sam Shepard's drama has grown in just over twenty years into a canon of plays that is rapidly approaching, in size and strength, the artistic achievement of those we consider this country's major playwrights. The list of major American playwrights is not very extensive, perhaps because American commercialism in the theatre inhibits the development of young playwrights. For whatever reason, Shepard's sustained achievement is indeed a rarity. With over forty plays to his credit, Shepard is among the most prolific playwrights to emerge from the Off-Off-Broadway movement. In these past two decades Shepard has demonstrated an extraordinary versatility, an openness to experimentation with dramatic forms, that also sets him apart from his contemporaries. Shepard's plays indicate his unwillingness to sacrifice form for content. "Ideas emerge from plays," he has said, "not the other way around."[45] Ideas or themes can indeed be extracted from Shepard's plays: the disintegration of the family, the betrayal of the American dream, the nostalgic lament for the loss of a mythic frontier, the deceptive lure of fame, wealth and power, the moral turpitude of personal relationships. But these tired expressions are not the plays themselves and serve mainly to reduce the vitality of Shepard's dramatic conceptions.

From his earliest experiments Shepard has sought a form to give expression to the fragmented images that gleam in his imagination. "It's almost as though the plays were a kind of chronical I was keeping on myself,"[46] he has said. Shepard's drama reflects his search for a way of rationalizing his experience; and his success attests to the far-reaching notes that that experience sounds. Shepard's imaginative expedition has led him through a variety of dramatic structures, each in its own way capturing a moment of thought evolving into action that can be relived and shared with an audience. Life spills out into his drama; and the theatrical conjoins with life. "Writing be-

comes more and more interesting as you go along," Shepard
says, "and it starts to open up some of its secrets. One thing
I'm sure of though. That I'll never get to the bottom of it."[47]
His dedication to developing and refining his art and his persistent exploration of the magic that can only be made in the
theatre are qualities to be cherished and nurtured by his audience.

Shepard's work remains experimental, as it must if it is to
continue to capture the imagination of the public. His plays
are, as he defines them himself, "risky," for "if there's no risk,
there's no experiment,"[48] and without experiment there is no
life in the drama. Although the Shepard hero has become a
recognizable character, he is still in process, still seeking his
way on uneasy terms with a mysterious world. The sense of
incompleteness that each of Shepard's plays leaves us with is
a welcome invitation to participate in an unfinished journey.
Shepard has said that he never knows how to end a play, that
he must finally stop so that people can leave the theatre. But
he refuses to impose form or enforce closure. "A resolution
isn't an ending," he says, "it's a strangulation."[49]

Shepard has answered America's need for a playwright whose
drama touches the depths of a nation's collective unconscious,
witnessed by his growing popularity and virtually unrivalled
success on the American stage. For the first twelve years of his
career, he resisted his earliest impulses to make the family the
center of his drama. While he remained outside the mainstream of American drama for over half his career, his later
plays have led him to the seemingly inevitable wide circle home
where, if anywhere, the answers to the questions his plays pose
may be found. In the path he has followed in search of himself,
Shepard's personal journey has led him through a myriad of
theatrical techniques and forms that he borrows from nearly
every major movement in contemporary theatre. And in doing
so, he has connected with a broad and varied audience as he
risks presenting his personal experience in universal forms. More
often than not he achieves his goal. "Hopefully, in writing a
play," Shepard says,

you can snare emotions that aren't just personal emotions, not just
catharsis, not just psychological emotions that you're getting off your

chest, but emotions and feelings that are connected with everybody. . . . But you start with something personal and see how it follows out and opens to something that's much bigger. That's what I'm
interested in.[50]

Like Artaud, Shepard tries to create "total theatre," theatre
that appeals to all the senses. His development as a writer,
however, has seemed to follow a direction opposite to Artaud's
hope for the drama. Rather than moving away from the social
and psychological Occidental theatre and toward the metaphysic of Oriental theatre, Shepard's drama has become increasingly psychosocial, particularly in the last ten years. Yet
everything that Shepard has to say about his drama indicates
his resistance to conceptualizing and his persistent effort to create a drama of images in space, a sensuous theatre that speaks
to the heart and not to the mind. Certainly the psychological
realism of his later plays is not of the kind that the American
theatre has grown accustomed to in the past. John Lion says of
Shepard's later work that he

presented a world which seems on the surface to make sense in the
traditional Western (read "Occidental") way, but on closer examination is seen to use the logic that we associate with realism and naturalism to show us that the world doesn't make sense, can never make
sense, will never make sense. Shepard did not "deconstruct" personality as some would claim—he *was* a deconstructed personality.[51]

Even in the later plays, Shepard's drama accomplishes what
Robert Brustein sees as Artaud's design: "to induce trance,
transport, and paroxysms by distilling the savagery of dreams
into the mystery of theatre."[52]

Wherever Shepard's restlessness may take him, we can be
sure that he will continue to express himself through art. "You
get to a certain point," he says, "and you want to *move*. I'd like
to do a lot of things. I'd like to do some sculpture. I'd like to
do some painting. Just to keep experimenting. Why not? Why
not try it all?"[53]

As long as Shepard continues to enjoy the mysteries of the
word's limitless potential, he will continue to astonish us with
plays that document his search for a form that can give ade-

quate expression to life. After borrowing and discarding the dramatic forms that historical criticism has neatly recorded, combining and reassembling them into novel shapes, Shepard may be at the apex of his career, a point in his development when his unique and individual talent may be poised to transcend tradition.

NOTES

1. Sam Shepard, "Metaphors, Mad Dogs, and Old-Time Cowboys," an interview with Kenneth Chubb *et al.*, *Theatre Quarterly*, 4, No. 15 (1974), p. 15.

2. *Ibid.*

3. Richard Gilman, "The Drama is Coming Now," in *The Modern American Theatre: A Collection of Critical Essays*, ed. Alvin B. Kernan (Englewood Cliffs, N. J.: Prentice–Hall Inc., 1967), p. 157.

4. Raymond Williams, *Drama from Ibsen to Brecht* (New York: Penguin Books, 1981), pp. 395–396.

5. Shepard, *Theatre Quarterly*, p. 8.

6. *Ibid.*, p. 15.

7. Bonnie Marranca, "Alphabetical Shepard: The Play of Words," in *American Dreams: The Imagination of Sam Shepard*, ed. Bonnie Marranca (New York: The Performing Arts Journal Press, 1981), p. 27.

8. Sam Shepard, *Curse of the Starving Class* in *Sam Shepard: Seven Plays* (New York: Bantam Books, 1981), pp. 174–75. All subsequent references cited in the text.

9. André Green, *The Tragic Effect*, trans. Alan Sheridan (Cambridge: Cambridge University Press, 1979), p. 2.

10. Benedict Nightingale, "Even Minimal Shepard is Food for Thought," *New York Times*, 25 September 1983, sec. 2, p. 5.

11. Jack Richardson, introduction, *Buried Child, Seduced, and Suicide in B♭* (New York: Urizen Books, 1979), ii.

12. Emile Zola, *The Experimental Novel and Other Essays*, trans. Belle M. Sherman (New York: Cassell Pub., 1983), reprinted in Bernard F. Dukore, ed., *Dramatic Theory and Criticism* (New York: Holt, Rinehart, and Winston, Inc., 1974), pp. 695–696.

13. Sam Shepard, *Buried Child* in *Sam Shepard: Seven Plays*, p. 91. Subsequent references cited in the text.

14. Mel Gussow, "The Deeply American Roots of Sam Shepard's Plays," *New York Times*, 2 January 1979, sec. 2, p. 1.

15. Richard Schechner, "Puzzling Pinter," *The Tulane Drama Review*, 11, No. 2 (Winter 1966), 176–185.

16. Harold Pinter, *The Homecoming* (New York: Grove Press, 1965), p. 41.

17. Schechner, "Pinter," p. 177.

18. Doris Auerbach, *Sam Shepard, Arthur Kopit, and the Off-Broadway Theater* (Boston: Twayne Publishers, 1982), p. 61.

19. Richard Gilman, introduction, *Sam Shepard: Seven Plays*, p. xxiv.

20. Bernard Weiner, "Shepard's Prize-Winning Nightmare at ACT," *San Francisco Chronicle*, 18 October 1979, p. 63.

21. Oscar G. Brockett, *History of the Theatre*, 2nd ed. (Boston: Allyn and Bacon Inc., 1974), p. 430.

22. Sam Shepard, *The Unseen Hand* in *The Unseen Hand and Other Plays* (New York: Urizen Books, 1972).

23. Sam Shepard, *The Sad Lament of Pecos Bill on the Eve of Killing His Wife* in *Theater*, 12, (Sum./Fall 1981), 32–38.

24. Sam Shepard, *True West* in *Sam Shepard: Seven Plays*, p. 6. Subsequent references cited in the text.

25. William Kleb, "Worse Than Being Homeless: *True West* and the Divided Self," in *American Dreams*, p. 124.

26. R. D. Laing, *The Divided Self* (New York: Penguin Books, 1969), p. 3.

27. Kleb, p. 124.

28. Tucker Orbison, "Mythic Levels and Shepard's *True West*," *Modern Drama*, Vol. xxvii, No. 4 (Dec. 1984), p. 515.

29. Henry Nash Smith, *Virgin Land: The American West as Symbol and Myth* (Cambridge, Mass.: Harvard University Press, 1950), p. 251.

30. Washington Irving, *Astoria, or Anecdotes of an Enterprise Beyond the Rocky Mountains*, 2 vols. (Philadelphia, 1836), I, 232.

31. Robert W. Corrigan, *The Theatre in Search of a Fix* (New York: Dell Publishing Co., 1973), p. 8.

32. *Ibid.*

33. Kleb, p. 121.

34. Frank Rich, "Stage: Sam Shepard's *True West*," *New York Times*, 24 December 1980, sec. 1., p. C9.

35. Sam Shepard, *Motel Chronicles* (San Francisco: City Lights, 1982), pp. 55–56.

36. Pete Hamill, "The New American Hero," an interview with Sam Shepard, *New York* (Dec. 1983), p. 80.

37. *Ibid.*

38. Edward Albee, *The Zoo Story* (New York: The New American Library Inc., 1959), p. 30.

39. Sam Shepard, *Fool for Love*, in *Fool for Love and Other Plays* (New York: Bantam Books, 1984), p. 27.

40. Nightingale, p. 26.

41. Sam Shepard, *A Lie of the Mind*. My reading is based on the preview performance of November 22, 1985 at the Promenade Theatre, New York City. Significant changes may have been made by opening night. *A Lie of the Mind* is unpublished.

42. *Ibid*.

43. *Ibid*.

44. Sam Shepard, as quoted by Samuel G. Freedman, "Sam Shepard and the Mythic Family," *New York Times*, 1 December 1985, sec. 2, p. 20, col. 3.

45. Sam Shepard, "Visualization, Language, and the Inner Library," in *Drama Review*, 21, No. 4 (Dec. 1977), p. 50.

46. *Ibid*. p. 58.

47. *Ibid*.

48. John Lion, "Rock 'n Roll Jesus with a Cowboy Mouth: Sam Shepard is the Inkblot of the '80s," *American Theatre*, 1, No. 1 (April 1984), p. 12.

49. *Ibid*., p. 11.

50. *Ibid*., p. 9.

51. *Ibid*., p. 8.

52. Robert Brustein, *The Theatre of Revolt* (Boston: Little Brown and Company, 1964), p. 375.

53. Robert Goldberg, "Sam Shepard, American Original," *Playboy*, 31 (March 1984), p. 193.

V

AFTERWORD: ON STAGE AND SCREEN

In the past few years Sam Shepard has become known to a wide audience as a film actor due largely to his popular roles in *Frances* (1982), *The Right Stuff* (1983), and *Country* (1984). His triumph on the screen is a possible source of alarm for critics who have witnessed too often in the past the loss of serious new artists to the lucrative film industry. Shepard assures us in a recent interview that he will remain principally a writer although he is not immune to the lure of the camera:

I'm a writer. The more I act, the more resistance I have to it. Now it seems to me that being an actor in films is like being sentenced to a trailer for twelve weeks . . . I don't like the kind of feeling of entrapment that you have to go through to make a film. . . . I don't know if I'll do it much longer.[1]

On the set of *Country*, in which he plays opposite Jessica Lange, with whom he costarred in *Frances*, Shepard says: "There's a definite fear about being diminished through film."[2] But, fully aware of the danger, he continues to subject himself to this odd form of self-imprisonment.

In Shepard's play *Angel City* (1976), he grotesquely parodies the Hollywood film industry. The main character, Rabbit Brown, is victimized and exploited by a rampant commercialism when he arrives to consult with producers Wheeler and Lanx, who imprison Rabbit in their self-sufficient "city" and force him to create an idea for their eight million dollar project. Rabbit and the musician Tympani are locked up together while they try to imagine a character to play the leading role in the greatest disaster film ever created. Wheeler, in the meantime, slowly becomes transformed into a slimy green monster with long fangs. His degeneration can only be halted by Rabbit's discovery of a "hard core disaster" that will liberate the producer. Finally, after mulling over many possibilities (death, plagues, global warfare), Rabbit discovers a solution. He occupies the producer's chair and when he swivels around to face the audience, Rabbit has become the producer—slimy green skin, fangs, and all. Wheeler screams hysterically for his identity to be returned, but Rabbit is now free and the tyrannical producer is trapped on the rectangular screen that hangs on the upstage wall. Rabbit tells Wheeler: "You're on the silver screen buddy. You've been captured in celluloid and you'll never get out."[3] Wheeler waves frantically at Lanx and his secretary Miss Scoons, but they only regard him as an image in a moving picture and continue munching calmly on their popcorn.

In spite of Shepard's dramatic allegory on the horrors of celluloid confinement, he has always been hypnotized by the film industry and the possibility for escape that movies offer. He remembers going to the movies when he was a child and "absolutely believing that this was a way to *be*. . . . It wasn't just an actor acting; this was a *life form*."[4] Shepard's fascination with the slim boundary between the character, on the stage or screen, and the reality of the actor who creates the role has been a major preoccupation of his as a writer and as an actor. In the playwright's collection of poems and narratives, *Motel Chronicles*, he records an experience on the set of the film *Resurrection*. As the actor in Shepard's story enters his mobile home—the trailer that he will be confined to for weeks—he finds his costume waiting for him and "it looked just like the clothes he had on, a deflated version of himself. He switched the clothes he had on for the costume and felt just the same. Exactly the same. Maybe a little bit stiffer. Cleaner maybe too. He wondered if he was supposed to be playing himself."[5] Then while shooting a motorcycle chase scene in which the character he portrays hunts down the woman he loved, he tries, as an actor, to understand what the scene is about: "He was supposed to be riding to kill her? The Star? The Character? The Woman?

The Character he was playing was supposed to be riding to kill the Character she was playing?"[6] As the actor ponders his role, he becomes oblivious to the signals of the director and cameraman and forgets about acting as he revels in the thrill of the chase and begins to ride his motorcycle dangerously fast. In the midst of his frenzied activity, "suddenly he appeared to himself. He caught himself in a flash. There was no more doubt who the Character was."[7]

By acting in films Shepard experiences first hand the situation he frequently creates for his dramatic characters—the task of finding themselves through role-playing. From the many parts he is offered, Shepard clearly selects those roles that have characteristics in common with his drama. He rejected an offer from Warren Beatty to play Eugene O'Neill in *Reds* thinking the role just a little "too cute"; he also turned down an opportunity to play the lead in *Urban Cowboy*. His first major role came in 1978 when Terence Malick cast him as the lonely young farmer in *Days of Heaven*, described by one critic as "a bleak and unstinting attack on America's materialistic culture."[8] Shepard's character is sympathetically portrayed as the victim of his own wealth and of the desperate plot of two migrant workers, Bill and Abby. Bill sees the opportunity to wed Abby to the farmer, who is terminally ill, and inherit his money. Abby, however, falls genuinely in love with the farmer; Bill kills his unwitting rival and is killed in turn by a vengeance-seeking posse. The melodramatic narrative is saved from complete bathos by the sweepingly beautiful cinematography and the slowly evolving images captured by the photographer. The film's images center around the farmer, a solitary figure isolated in his mid-Victorian clapboard house, a lonely man surrounded by wide expanses of wheat fields that extend to the limits of the horizon. Stanley Kauffmann found one redeeming feature in the film, Shepard's "lean and troubled face [that] brings this picture as close as it ever gets to drama."[9]

The desolation that accompanies great wealth is the subject of Shepard's play *Seduced* (1979) which dramatizes the last day in the life of Henry Hackamore, a dramatic surrogate of Howard Hughes. Like the farmer in *Days of Heaven*, Hackamore is seduced and sequestered by his wealth. He has built "an entire legacy on nothin' but air."[10] Hackamore has a recurring vision of himself, "alone. Standing in Open country . . . enormous, primitive country, . . . Flat, Barren, Wasted" (p. 111). Shepard thus creates an image in his film role that corresponds quite closely to one of his fully developed dramatic characters.

In *Resurrection* (1980) Shepard plays the rebellious son of a small-town minister who falls in love with Edna Mae (Ellen Burstyn), a woman who has survived a near-fatal accident and acquired the gift of faith-healing. Edna Mae's irreverent attitude toward her gift arouses her young lover's fury. Unable to escape his fundamentalist background, Shepard's character demands that Edna Mae attribute her miracles to God (she gives love, not God, credit), and when she refuses he threatens her life. Shepard's screen portrayal of a young man who is isolated from the life of the small town in which he was brought up builds primarily from a reactionary attitude toward his religious–zealot father. The character in *Days of Heaven* discovers, however, that in critical moments the father's values that he rejects resurface to govern his own action. Shepard dramatizes this conflict in all five of his naturalistic plays when Wesley, Vince, Austin, Lee, Eddie, and Jake enact a similar struggle with the psychological ghosts of their fathers.

In *Frances* (1982) Shepard plays Harry York, a left-wing journalist who remains faithfully in love with actress Frances Farmer (Jessica Lange) as he follows her tragic career from the sidelines. York shows up each time Farmer experiences a crisis in her life and is abandoned by her family and friends. Although York voices his own political opinions cautiously, he clearly sympathizes with and admires the outspoken Farmer whose differences of opinion with the world in general mark her as a menace to society from the point of view of those who cannot tolerate too many truths loudly spoken. York is an outsider and an observer, a man who watches Farmer's drama unfold with care and pity, but can never fully become a part of her life, can never take control of the action.

As an actor, Shepard received the most attention for his portrayal of Chuck Yeager in *The Right Stuff*. Shepard's appeal has much to do with an aloof, laconic, distanced attitude that he easily conveys. Yeager was, of course, the first test pilot to break the sound barrier; but his remarkable achievement was eclipsed by the success of the Mercury astronauts. In the film, Shepard's Yeager stands apart from the group of seven astronauts, an insular figure who represents a past when one man could conquer a territory alone. Yeager's solo flights are presented in sharp contrast to the massive machinery that comprised the first shuttle launches.

Shepard's heroes, on both the stage and screen, are often at odds with a world in which they find themselves to be strangers, spiritually, emotionally, or psychologically outcast. Often they belong to a forgotten past, or a yet–to–be–realized future. If Chuck Yeager is Shepard's finest screen performance, it is perhaps because he most fully embodies the typical hero of a Shepard play. In Colin Wilson's study of the alienation of modern man, *The Outsider*, the author repeatedly searches for a metaphor or a model that might crystallize the outsider's peculiar nature. In his postscript, Wilson discovers an analogy that figuratively conveys the outsider's problem.

When aviation experts perfected a plane that was capable of breaking the sound barrier there remained a problem: the planes tended to enter a steep dive, crashing when the pilot pulled back harder on the stick. "And then one day," Wilson says, "an exceptionally gifted test pilot tried doing something absurd. Instead of frantically pulling back on the stick, he tried pushing it forward—which logically ought to have made the dive steeper than ever. Instead the plane straightened out. At speeds greater than that of sound, some of the usual laws of nature get reversed. This, it seemed to me, is a picture of the 'outsider problem.' "[11]

Wilson, of course, refers to Chuck Yeager in this passage. His outsiders constitute a tiny minority, among them the artists who live a life of the mind, who do not need other people to express their dominance but who rather "explore the world of their own being."[12] Shepard is drawn to the portrayal of "outsiders," characters whose worlds are confined only by the limits of their own imagination.

Since his unsatisfying work on *Zabriskie Point* (1969), Shepard has shied away from screenwriting. But in 1984 he ventured again into the genre in collaboration with Wim Wenders, the famous German film director, known for his preoccupation with American "road pictures." The result of their collaboration, *Paris, Texas*, won the Palme d'Or at the 1984 Cannes Film Festival. *Paris, Texas* opens with a panoramic view of Shepard's fondest landscape as the camera hovers over "a fissured, empty, almost lunar landscape—seen from a bird's-eye view,"[13] Devil's Graveyard, Big Bend, Texas. Loping across this desert with his eyes fixed firmly though vacuously ahead is Travis Henderson (Harry Dean Stanton), the film's hero and by now the recognizable quintessential Shepardian hero. Travis is wearing a cheap pin-striped suit, red tie, red baseball cap, and sandals wrapped with bandages. His only company is a hawk that lands on a boulder to watch this man's aimless trek. Travis is covered with dust and sweat; he has been walking for a long time. He could easily be a younger version of the father in any of Shepard's last five plays. This anomic scene projects the destiny that we suspect any one of Shepard's later heroes may succumb to. It is the likely fate of Weston in *Curse of the Starving Class*; it is the imaginary space out of which Lee emerges and will return in *True West*; it is a macrocosmic view of the barren garden in *Buried Child*; and it is the wide expanse of nothingness that surrounds Eddie and May in *Fool for Love*.

Andrew Kopkind, in his review of the film, recognizes in *Paris, Texas* "the tension between two completely dissimilar brothers, which Shepard used in *True West* to illustrate the unfinished American war of gentility against violence, remembrance against forgetting, cities against plains, the present against the past."[14] Like Lee in *True West*, Travis is a renegade and a desperado; like Austin, Walt is a quasi-artist and successful urban professional. Travis has been absent from society for four years, living a never-to-be-explained existence in a world far removed from the billboards his brother designs that dot the Los Angeles freeways. In a sense, *Paris, Texas* conflates the prominent themes of *True West* and *Fool for Love*. The latter play was Shepard's first serious excursion into the perplexities of male/female relationships. Until he wrote *Fool for Love*, Shepard's primary fascination was with relationships between men, mainly fathers and sons. In *Fool for Love* he set out deliberately to create a fully autonomous female character, one who could "remain absolutely true to herself, not only as a social being, but also as an emotional being."[15] At this point in his career, Shepard realized that his previous assumption that there is "more mystery to relationships between men" was not true, that he could find "the same mystery between men and women."[16] The principle narrative line in *Paris, Texas* concerns the mysterious separation of Travis and Jane Henderson and leads to Travis's implementation of a reunion between Jane and their eight-year-old son Hunter.

Walter rescues Travis from a rather maniacal doctor at the Terlingua Medical Clinic where his brother has collapsed. He takes him home, reunites him with his son, whom Walt and his wife have kept since Travis and Jane's disappearance four years before, and nurtures him back to health. Once recovered, Travis goes back on the road, this time accompanied by his son, in search of his wife Jane (Nastassja Kinski). The climactic scene occurs in an onanistic peep-show where Travis finds Jane working in a small cubicle with one–way mirrors. Travis can see Jane and speak to her on a telephone; Jane can only see her own reflection in the mirror that separates and protects her from her clients. In this setting Travis narrates the story of his passionate love for his young wife that turned into jealous obsession and ended in violence. For a few moments, the couple are reunited to share their story, as Eddie and May are in *Fool for Love*; like the dramatic couple, Travis and Jane can share a mutual understanding of the obvious reasons for their conflict, but cannot uncover the deeper truths that might permit reconciliation. In the last scene of *Paris, Texas*, Travis drives away from the hotel where his wife and son are joyously reunited. In the rearview mirror of his pickup truck he stares stony-faced at his own image, which softens gradually into an expression that mingles despair with acceptance.

Paris, Texas in part may reflect Shepard's own pain about his divorce from O-Lan, his wife for over fifteen years. In a press interview he talked of "the idea that there's an imaginary part-

ner and an imaginary life that's always superseding the real
one. . . . In this relationship between men and women, two
things are always in juxtaposition with each other: you know,
the idea of who I'm with, and who I'm actually with."[17]

Shepard describes the "true relationship" between men and
women as "terrible and impossible."[18] But Shepard's primary
interest is still with the father figure. In an 1984 interview he
spoke of a screenplay he was writing called *Synthetic Tears*, about
a son's attempt to restore his alcoholic father to the family. He
said of this work–in–progress: "it encompasses a whole period
of my life that I had never been able to synthesize, that I had
always struggled with."[19] And he speaks of his own father's
anger:

My father had a real short fuse. He had a really rough life—had to
support his mother and brothers at a very young age when his dad's
farm collapsed. You could see his suffering, his terrible suffering, living a life that was disappointing and looking for another one. It was
past frustration, it was anger. My father was full of terrifying anger.[20]

In Shepard's film adaptation of *Fool for Love* he plays one of his
own characters, Eddie. Not since 1971, when he took the role
of Slim in the American Place Theatre's production of *Cowboy
Mouth*, has Shepard combined his talents as writer and actor in
the same play. Perhaps Shepard is approaching a time when
he can, in reality, play all the parts.

Despite Shepard's insistence that he has no interest in psychological studies of character, his last few plays, his first successful screenplay, and his screenplay in progress all suggest a
movement toward deeper exploration of family connections,
particularly in response to the son's unresolved conflict with
the father and the effect of this irresolution on the son's love
relationships. Whether his medium is the stage or the screen,
we can expect that Shepard will continue to investigate these
fundamental bonds in search of the heart of the mystery. The
recent death of his father may make the effort to resolve the
conflict even more insistent. Shepard's hope to write the defin-
itive piece, the "one play that will end [his] need to write plays"
has not been realized.[21] His disappointment in failing to reach

"the depths of certain emotional territory"[22] is the American theatre's promise that Shepard will continue to offer plays and films that probe the American psyche.

NOTES

1. Pete Hamill, "The New American Hero," an interview with Sam Shepard, *New York* (Dec. 1982), p. 102.

2. *Ibid.*, p. 100.

3. Sam Shepard, *Angel City* in *Angel City, Curse of the Starving Class, and Other Plays* (New York: Urizen Press, 1976), p. 52.

4. Hamill, p. 84.

5. Sam Shepard, *Motel Chronicles* (San Francisco: City Lights, 1982), p. 11.

6. *Ibid.*, p. 12.

7. *Ibid.*, p. 13.

8. Frank Rich, "Night of the Locust," *Time*, 18 September 1978, p. 93.

9. Stanley Kauffmann, "Harder Times," *The New Republic*, 16 September 1978, p. 17.

10. Sam Shepard, *Seduced* in *Buried Child, Seduced and Suicide in B♭* (New York: Urizen Books, 1979), p. 101. Subsequent references cited in the text.

11. Colin Wilson, *The Outsider* (New York: Bell Publishing Co., 1956), p. 296.

12. *Ibid.*, p. 298.

13. Sam Shepard, *Paris, Texas* (Berlin: Road Movies, 1984), p. 7.

14. Andrew Kopkind, "Countrification," *The Nation*, V. 239, 27 October 1984, p. 426.

15. Sam Shepard, as quoted by Michiko Kakutani, "Myths, Dreams, Realities—Sam Shepard's America," *New York Times*, 29 January 1984, sec. 2, p. 17.

16. *Ibid.*

17. Sam Shepard, as quoted by Blanche McCrary Boyd, "Sam Shepard—Playwright, Actor, Man in Love," *Cosmopolitan*, V. 239, 29 December 1984, p. 65.

18. Sam Shepard, as quoted by Stephen Fay, "the silent type," *Vogue*, V. 213, February 1985, p. 216.

19. Sam Shepard, as quoted by Robert Goldberg, "Sam Shepard, American Original," *Playboy*, V. 31, March 1984, p. 193.

20. *Ibid.*, p. 191.

21. Fay, p. 218.

22. *Ibid.*

CHRONOLOGY OF A CAREER

Samuel Shepard Rogers Jr. was born on November 5, 1943 in Fort Sheridan, Illinois, "a real fort where army mothers had their babies."[1] His father was an army officer whose career took the family from Rapid City, South Dakota, to Utah, to Florida. The Shepards' last military-based home was on Guam, which left Shepard with the striking images he would later recall in his book of short stories, monologues, and poems, *Hawk Moon*:

A jeep bounces violently through lush jungle green hanging wet dripping plants with snakes. The mother fires four from her revolver out the window through the thick rain, the kid on the floor in a cowboy hat covering his ears.[2]

The Japanese on Guam crept down from the villages to steal clothes from his mother's clothesline, which she defended with an army-issued luger. He called them "gooks" like all the other kids; "it wasn't until the Viet Nam War that I realized 'gook' was a derogatory term."[3] When his father retired from the army, the family went to live with an aunt in South Pasadena, California where his mother, Jane (Schook) Rogers, taught elementary school children and his father attended night classes to complete his bachelor's degree. Shepard remembers his father as a strict disciplinarian in regard to studying, and consequently he developed an early dislike for "writing in notebooks—it was really like being jailed."[4] But he shared his father's love for Dixieland jazz and soon surpassed his father's accomplishment on drums.

When Shepard was about twelve years old the family moved to an avocado ranch in Duarte, California. Here he developed a love for farming, and the close contact with the animals on the ranch fostered in him a desire to become a veterinarian. A 4-H club member, Shepard even had a prize ram at the Los Angeles County Fair one year. It was here also that he remembers awakening to the social stratification and injustice of small-town America. The "wrong side of the tracks" was a literal reality in this small southern California community where the blacks and the Mexicans were separated from the white community by the railroad tracks that divided Duarte. The friends that Shepard made in Duarte High School would later serve as models for some of the playwright's most memorable characters. There was the Elvis Presley look-alike who wore flashy clothes and greased his long black hair, a standout in the crowd of clean-cut ivy league boys wearing button–down collars and penny loafers. The "computer freaks" who worked at the aeronautics plant and bought fancy cars and amphetamines with money from stolen parts also left an array of indelible images in Shepard's mind. In his last years of high school Shepard worked as a stable hand at the Conley Arabian Horse Ranch in Chino, California. Later Shepard would recall some of his adolescent adventures, stealing goose eggs and goat's milk from the Los Angeles County Fair, getting stoned on Benzedrine and driving his Renault Dauphine, stealing a car in Pasadena, watching Leo Carillo, the Lone Ranger, and Hop-along Cassidy riding in the Rose Parade, "cruising Bob's Big Boy . . . looking for chicks."[5]

In 1961 Shepard enrolled at Mount Antonio Junior College only to drop out one year later to join the Bishop's Repertory Company, a religious-oriented acting troupe that played one–night church stops. In a 1984 interview Shepard remembers his first experience with a theatre troupe:

We'd go into churches, mostly in New England, set up lights, do make-up, do the play, tear it all down and leave to go down the road the next day. It really gave you a sense of the makeshift quality of theater and the possibilities of doing it anywhere. That's what turned me on most of all. I realized suddenly that anybody can make theater.[6]

Persistent problems at home and the lure of the Beat generation enticed Shepard to remain in New York when the troupe
stopped there. Nineteen years old, he arrived in New York's
Lower East Side village where an old high school friend, Charles
Mingus Jr., a painter and son of the jazz musician, helped him
secure a job as a busboy at a nightclub called the Village Gate.
Stimulated by the sights and sensations of this electrifying, alien
environment, Shepard felt compelled to write about it. After a
brief, unsuccessful attempt to become an actor in New York,
an experience he equated with "being a hooker,"[7] he began
writing poetry. He also dropped his original surname of Rogers
and adopted the shortened name, Sam Shepard. As a boy he
had been nicknamed "Steve" to distinguish him from his father. Years later he would learn that "Steve Rogers" was the
name of the original "Captain America" of the comics.

Ralph Cook, then head waiter at the Village Gate, had just
acquired some space in St. Mark's Church in-the-Bouwerie,
which he planned to use as a theatre. Elenore Lester of the *New
York Times* described this new environment at Tenth Street and
Second Avenue:

the winos stumble along streets filled with racially mixed couples, young
drop-outs from the affluent suburbs and long-haired young men
wearing incredibly narrow jeans and brass-buttoned Civil War jackets,
the plays reflect something of the Dostoevskian anguish of a generation afflicted with a sense of menace and crisis.[8]

Looking for new material, Cook encouraged Shepard to abandon poetry and turn to writing plays. With one playwriting
attempt behind him, a self-professed "very bad play, a sort of
Tennessee Williams imitation," Shepard wrote two one-acts for
Cook, *Cowboys* and *The Rock Garden*.[9] The latter grew out of his
feelings about leaving his California home. The former concerns one of Shepard's persistent fantasies and dramatic preoc-
cupations. He recalls 1963 in New York City, running around
the streets with Charles, "playing cowboys . . . in the midst
of all these people who were going to work and riding the
buses."[10] Ralph Cook remembers how Shepard would jump
onto the hood of a cab that refused to stop and ride it cowboy
style down the block.[11]

Shepard's two one-acts constituted the first bill at Cook's new theatre in St. Mark's, Theatre Genesis. Critics like Jerry Talmer of the *Post* blasted Shepard's first efforts as solely derivative of Beckett. Disturbed and disheartened, the novice playwright was on the verge of returning to California. But Michael Smith of the *Village Voice* also attended Theatre Genesis's opening and his review sounded the approval and encouragement Shepard needed. Theatre Genesis boasted a dedication to the new playwright and Smith acknowledged: "it sounds pretentious and unprepossessing . . . but they have actually found a new playwright [who] has written a pair of provocative and genuinely original plays."[12] Smith felt certain that Shepard had been aware of European models for his work but found his voice to be "distinctly American and his own."[13] Shepard insisted that he knew only Beckett's *Waiting for Godot*, and claimed that he liked it but really did not know what to make of it. Nevertheless, Smith's support brought audiences into Theatre Genesis and Shepard began writing almost as quickly as the Off-Off-Broadway playhouses could accommodate his work.

Four new plays appeared early the next year. La Mama's Experimental Theatre Club produced *Rocking Chair* and *Dog* (unpublished plays that Shepard scarcely remembers) in February 1965; *Up to Thursday* and *4-H Club* shared the Cherry Lane Theatre's New Playwrights Series bill for 1965 with Paul Foster's *Balls* and Lanford Wilson's *Home Free!* In April of that year Theatre Genesis staged *Chicago* and Michael Smith once again praised "Shepard's precise vision and ebullient sense of life's fullness."[14] Smith's enthusiasm led him to direct Shepard's next play, *Icarus' Mother*, which opened at the Caffe Cino on November 16, 1965. Edward Albee joined his voice with theatre critics who were beginning to notice "the youngest and most gifted of the new playwrights working Off-Broadway," despite the fact that Albee thought the production of *Icarus' Mother* was a dreadful mess.[15] In one year Shepard had six new plays produced, purportedly written because "there was nothing else to do."[16] In a recent interview, Shepard describes his self-discovery as a writer in a characteristically rural metaphor: "It was as though somebody was stuck somewhere and had nothing to do but whittle on a piece of wood, and all of a sudden discovered he could make sculpture."[17] There was no remuneration for these early plays, so Shepard continued to work as a waiter at Marie's Crisis Cafe.

In January of 1966 *Red Cross* opened at the Judson Poet's Theatre and won Shepard his first Obie award. In April Tom O'Horgan revived *Chicago* in "Six From La Mama" at the Off-Broadway Martinique Theatre. Stanley Kauffmann described this "anti-play" as a "free-flowing, salty, and touching little rhapsody on a small incident seen through the prism of fancy."[18] Another new play, *Fourteen Hundred Thousand*, moved outside of New York to be presented by the Firehouse Theatre in Minneapolis. The same year *Chicago* and *Icarus' Mother* were also cited for Obie awards, making Shepard the first playwright to receive three Obies in one year.

Nineteen sixty–seven was an important year in Shepard's career. In March, his first full-length play, *La Turista*, was produced by the American Place Theatre. Ellen Stewart took her La Mama troupe on tour in Europe and in their September season at London's Mercury Theatre Shepard's *Chicago* and *Melodrama Play* were offered. *Cowboys #2*, a rewrite of the lost original *Cowboys*, opened on August 12 at New York's Old Reliable Theatre and in November moved to the West coast to play at Los Angeles's Mark Taper Forum. Theatre Genesis once again presented a new Shepard play, *Forensic and the Navigators*, on December 29. *Forensic* began in rehearsal as a five-page scenario which grew and developed as the cast rehearsed. A young actress, O-Lan Johnson, who auditioned for the made-to-order part of Oolan, married Shepard two years later. Shepard's continuing interest in music expressed itself in this new play. A rock concert followed the production and the author made an appearance as drummer for the Moray Eels. *Forensic and the Navigators* and *La Turista* added two more Obies to the playwright's growing collection.

Other interests were made public in 1967 with the production of Shepard's first screenplay, *Me and My Brother*, about Peter Orlovsky, written for Robert Frank. Shepard had previously written two screenplays that were never produced, *Maxagasm*, written for Mick Jagger, and *The Bodyguard* (with Tony Richardson), an adaptation of the Jacobean tragedy *The Change-*

ling. Another opportunity arose for Shepard to continue his interest in film. A production of *Icarus' Mother* caught the attention of the great Italian director Michelangelo Antonioni who solicited Shepard's assistance for his new film *Zabriskie Point* (released by MGM in 1969). Shepard left for Rome to offer his services as an advisor for Antonioni's denunciation of American consumption-obsessed society. The film was badly received by the critics and Shepard's contribution remains rather nebulous, but the whole experience left the twenty-four-year-old playwright exhausted and debilitated. The next time he would venture into the arena of film it would be as an actor. But the events of 1967 brought Shepard much recognition and at last financial support began to pour in. Fellowships from the University of Minnesota, Yale, and a Rockefeller Grant put an end to Shepard's work at the Hickory House Restaurant in New York.

The next year brought another grant, from the Guggenheim Foundation, and another Obie award for *Melodrama Play.* Nineteen sixty–nine was the year of *Oh Calcutta!* and Sam Shepard's name was among the formidable list of contributors. His early one-act, *The Rock Garden,* was incorporated into Kenneth Tynan's landmark revue. Also that year, the first of Shepard's plays to be televised, *Fourteen Hundred Thousand,* was produced by National Educational Television's Playhouse Program. Prolific as ever, Shepard presented the public with three new plays in 1969, *Shaved Splits, The Unseen Hand,* and *The Holy Ghostly,* the latter two selected by La Mama's New Troupe Branch tour of 1969. In March, London's Royal Court Theatre produced *La Turista* at their Theatre Upstairs. On November 9, 1969, Shepard and O-Lan Johnson, the Off-Broadway actress who played Oolan in *Forensic and the Navigators,* were married. The wedding ceremony took place fittingly at St. Mark's Church in-the-Bouwerie, the home of Theatre Genesis. The couple had one child, a son, Jesse Mojo.

In 1970 Shepard faced what appears to be an inevitable dilemma for young American playwrights. The Vivian Beaumont Theatre at New York's Lincoln Center wanted to produce Shepard's new play, *Operation Sidewinder,* which demanded a technically lavish set and therefore a strong financial backing. The

choice was unusual for the Lincoln Center, which is not nota-
ble for venturing into the world premieres of unknown plays
by little–known playwrights. And the decision was a difficult
one for Shepard, who is known for his resistance to large-scale
productions with heavy critical coverage. He had made a small
stir in 1967 when he became the first playwright to exercise the
American Place Theatre's option to bar critics from their production of *La Turista*. Objecting to the American system of
judging success or failure on the basis of income and widespread appeal, Shepard was offended by critics who sat in
judgment, some with the power to close plays with their opinion. But there was no Off–Off–Broadway theatre with financial
resources capable of staging *Operation Sidewinder*. The production was undertaken and Shepard again appeared as a drummer, this time for the Holy Modal Rounders who performed to
cover scene changes. The expensive mechanical sidewinder, an
elaborate prop designed by John Delasser that suggested both
its definitions of a desert rattlesnake and a heat-seeking air–
to–air missile, apparently stole the show; it would be some years
before Shepard would once again venture too far from Off–
Off–Broadway. Meanwhile, in April of 1970, New York's Astor
Place Theatre presented *The Unseen Hand* and *Forensic and the
Navigators* on a double bill. In August, Shepard's durable *Cowboys #2* kept company with Strindberg's *The Stronger* and
Ionesco's *The New Tenant* at the Old Post Office Theatre on Long
Island. In the spring of 1970 Shepard appeared in *Brand X*, directed by Win Chamberlain. Penelope Gilliatt of the *New Yorker*
described the film as "a filthy, good-humored, crass, . . .
something–or–other that derides the America of advertising and
flag–waving."[19]

The next year Shepard returned to Off–Off–Broadway with
three new plays. In April of 1971 Shepard's *Cowboy Mouth*,
coauthored with the rock artist and singer Patti Smith, played
at the American Place Theatre along with another new play,
Back Bog Beast Bait. *Cowboy Mouth* was also presented by Edinburgh's Traverse Theatre, and London's Open Space Theatre
produced *Icarus' Mother*. In March, O-Lan Shepard took the role
of Mae West in her husband's new production at Theatre Genesis, *The Mad Dog Blues*.

A short time later Shepard left New York with his wife and son to settle for a few years in Hampstead, London. In these years Shepard would begin to capture the interest and win the admiration of English directors, actors, and audiences, much as he had done in New York. The reputation that went before him was not terribly positive. When Shepard's *Red Cross* reached London by way of the New York Workshop's tour in 1970, it failed to impress and succeeded in confusing the English audience. Irving Wardle of the *Times* commented, "it makes no conceptual sense and you feel it was damned easy to write," but he conceded, "unlike most easy writing it plays extremely well."[20] Shepard's work was represented by the Open Theatre's 1971–72 season at London's Roundhouse, which included two plays, *Nightwalk* and *Terminal*, on which he collaborated with other members of the Open Theatre's ensemble including Megan Terry and Jean-Claude Van Itallie. But it was the summer of 1972 when Shepard was significantly recognized with five plays on London stages: *Red Cross, Cowboy Mouth*, and *Chicago* at the King's Head; *Cowboy #2* at the Pindar of Wakefield; and *The Tooth of Crime* at the Open Space, directed by Charles Marowitz. *The Unseen Hand* followed the next year at the Royal Court's Theatre Upstairs, and *The Holy Ghostly* played in July at the King's Head. In the spring of 1973 the BBC broadcast Shepard's *Blue Bitch*, an unpublished play about expatriate Americans (Dixie and Cody) living in London. A Shepard import, *The Tooth of Crime*, was brought to the Cambridge Street Theatre in Edinburgh by Richard Schechner's Performance Group after receiving its premiere at the McCarter Theatre in Princeton. This last play marked a turning point in critical opinion about Shepard's work. Representative of this changing attitude is Clive Barnes's *New York Times* review of the Princeton production. Barnes had followed Shepard's career for several years with cautious approval, but now he abandoned his reticence to say without his usual qualifications: "Sam Shepard is a young American playwright of pure brilliance and imaginative fantasy."[21] The following year *The Tooth of Crime* was revived by the Royal Court, and two new plays, *Geography of a Horse Dreamer* and *Action* were produced by the same company. In March of 1974 the Hampstead Theatre Club produced *Little Ocean*, an unpublished series of sketches in which three women offer various attitudes toward pregnancy and childbirth. Shepard continued to demonstrate his versatility by publishing *Hawk Moon*, his first collection of stories and poems.

Now Shepard was ready to return to America. He did so to find himself the recipient of two more Obie awards for *Action* and *The Tooth of Crime*, and hailed by the *New York Times* as one of America's most important young playwrights since Edward Albee.[22] In 1976 Shepard again entered into a new field when he wrote *The Sad Lament of Pecos Bill on the Eve of Killing His Wife*, a one-act opera written for the Bay Area Playwright's Festival. In October, a new play, *Suicide in B♭*, was presented by the Yale Repertory Theatre. At the twentieth annual presentation of Creative Arts Medals by Brandeis University, Shepard received the award for Achievement in Theatre. Meanwhile, in 1976, Shepard found time to join Bob Dylan and Allen Ginsberg on their Rolling Thunder Tour. Asked to accompany the group as a scriptwriter for a film that was never completed, Shepard did keep a travel journal, published by the Viking Press as *The Rolling Thunder Logbook*, in the words of the author, "a fractured" account of the tour designed "just to give the reader a taste of the whole experience."[23] Shepard continued his relationship with Dylan in 1977 when he wrote some of the dialogue for and played the role of Rodeo in Dylan's screenplay *Renaldo and Clara*.

Since his return from England, Shepard had been disturbed by the difficulty of having his plays produced in New York in circumstances he found suitable. Since his early intimacy with Theatre Genesis he had longed for a close and continuing relationship with a theatre dedicated to experiment and development of the art form. Returning to the West coast he approached San Francisco's American Conservatory Theatre, who could only offer him a few workshop performances in their basement. But the Magic Theatre, a group that produced *La Turista* in 1970, welcomed Shepard's *Action* and *Killer's Head* with the playwright directing in the spring of 1975. At the same time the American Place Theatre produced these two plays in New York. A new play, *Angel City*, followed, and the Magic Theatre became the home for most of Shepard's opening plays.

Following a now well-established tradition, *Angel City* moved from the Magic Theatre to the East coast, in this instance to Princeton's McCarter Theatre, in the spring of 1977. In the basement of the large warehouse at Fort Mason on San Francisco Bay, Shepard finally had his workshop theatre with a small group of dedicated actors. Since *Forensic and the Navigators*, Shepard had been interested in developing a script collaboratively in rehearsal as a process of discovery. Supported by a Rockefeller Grant he now had the opportunity, resulting in *Inacoma*, an exploration of the mind in coma-related visions, which opened at the Magic Theatre on March 18, 1977. And his new play for 1977, *Curse of the Starving Class*, which premiered at London's Royal Court Theatre in April, won him yet another Obie award in the midst of much controversy as it was the first play to be recognized as the best new American play of the season though it was not produced in New York until March 2, 1978 by the New York Shakespeare Festival.

On June 27, 1978 *Buried Child* premiered at the Magic Theatre. From there it moved to New York's Theatre de Lys where it played 152 performances. In 1979, Shepard was awarded the Pulitzer Prize for *Buried Child*. Another first for Shepard, *Buried Child* was the first Pulitzer–winning play that had never received a Broadway production. It also won the playwright a record-breaking tenth Obie award. Again exploring new territory, Shepard wrote the libretto *Jacaranda* for Daniel Nagrin. This stream–of–consciousness monologue of lost love was produced by Playhouse 46 in St. Clements Church. In the fall of 1978 Shepard appeared in Terence Malick's film *Days of Heaven*, in which he played a solitary Texas farmer who falls victim to his own innocence. Reviews of the film were mixed but Shepard's performance was highly praised. One critic who did not enjoy the film thought Shepard's "lean and troubled face brings this picture as close as it ever gets to drama."[24]

In February of 1979 another new play was produced by the American Place Theatre, *Seduced*, an imaginary biography of the last day in the life of Howard Hughes. In the fall of that year Shepard collaborated with Joseph Chaikin on *Savage/Love* and *Tongues*, described as "environments where the words and gestures are given temporary atmospheres to breathe in."[25] Following a brief run at the summer Eureka Festival and the Magic Theatre in California, these plays were produced by Joseph Papp at the Public Theatre in New York.

Shepard's relationship with Papp became the subject of controversy when his next full-length play, *True West*, moved from the Magic Theatre where it premiered on July 10, 1980, to Papp's Public Theatre. Problems arose between Papp and Robert Woodruff who frequently directs Shepard's plays in San Francisco. Woodruff resigned; Papp took over as director; the critics denounced the production; and Shepard vowed never again to allow one of his plays to be produced by Papp. *True West* has since been produced by New York's Cherry Lane Theatre where it became the longest-running Shepard play in New York when it closed in August of 1984 after ten previews and 762 performances. England's National Theatre also produced this play in the fall of 1981. In the fall of 1980 Shepard again appeared on the screen opposite Ellen Burstyn in Lewis John Carlino's *Resurrection*. Once again Shepard, as Burstyn's lover, a man haunted by his fundamentalist past, received especially fine reviews. Richard Corliss of *Time* said "his whip-thin body coils itself around a character . . . he menaces and mesmerizes." [26]

Shepard's plays continued to be produced actively both in America and abroad. By the winter of 1980, Shepard was "the second most produced playwright in the country (after Tennessee Williams)." [27] La Mama E.T.C. presented a Shepard double bill in September 1983: Shepard's "country opera," *The Sad Lament of Pecos Bill on the Eve of Killing His Wife*, with O-Lan Shepard as Sluefoot Sue; and *Superstitions*, a pastiche of sketches from *Motel Chronicles*. La Mama also revived *The Tooth of Crime* in a splendid production in the winter of 1983, and at the same time *Action* was presented on a double bill with Ionesco's *The Lesson* at the Collective Actors Theatre in New York.

In 1981, Shepard took the role of Bailey in Jack Fisk's *Raggedy Man*. The part had almost no dialogue, a fact which intrigued Shepard, who said during the filming:

It's a real challenge. I want to do a kind of Japanese character with this guy. Like the Kurosawa films where characters are like apparitions. They don't speak but they have this whole physical thing. [28]

At this point in Shepard's career as an actor, one critic saw him, "if he wants it, . . . on the brink of an extraordinary new career in the movies."[29] But Shepard insisted: "I'm not at all interested in becoming a movie star. What interests me is working with film artists."[30]

In the spring of 1983 Shepard played Harry York opposite Jessica Lange in *Frances*, the screen biography of actress Frances Farmer. *Fool for Love* closed in April 1983 after a limited engagement at the San Francisco Magic Theatre. A month later, *Fool for Love* reopened at New York's Circle Repertory Theatre where it played for over a year and was awarded an Obie for the best new American play of the 1983–84 season. In the fall of 1983 Shepard appeared in *The Right Stuff*, an adaptation of Thomas Wolfe's novel about the new frontier exploration of the American astronauts. Shepard was nominated for an Academy award as best supporting actor for his portrayal in the film of Chuck Yeager, the man who broke the sound barrier. Shepard's next film role was in *Country* (1984) where he again costarred with Jessica Lange with whom he now lives in Santa Fe, New Mexico. Not since *Zabriskie Point* has Shepard been involved in a screenplay that overtly addresses contemporary social issues. *Country*, a film about a couple who nearly lose their farm in their confrontation with insensitive bureaucracies, reached most American theatres in the fall of 1984, an election year when the plight of American farmers was a hotly debated issue. Cast as a farmer who resorts to drinking to mute the pain of losing his farm to merciless corporate strategy, Shepard's character strikes out at his wife and son in a violent expression of his helplessness. The role is one that must have intrigued Shepard, who admits his fascination with violence and the socialization of the American male:

I think there's something about American violence that to me is very touching. In full force, it's very ugly, but there's also something very moving about it because it has to do with humiliation. There's some hidden, deeply rooted thing in the Anglo male American that has to do with inferiority, that has to do with not being a man, and always, continually having to act out some idea of manhood that invariably is violent.[31]

This sympathy for the aggressiveness of American men is certainly a major preoccupation for Shepard, one that he explores deeply through the character of Eddie in *Fool for Love* and Jake in *A Lie of the Mind*. Shepard's film adaptation of *Fool for Love* stars Harry Dean Stanton as the old man and Shepard himself as Eddie.

In 1984, Joseph Chaikin and Shepard were collaborating on a new play, *The War in Heaven*, about a fallen angel who is interrogated on earth.[32] When I talked with Chaikin he was considering who would carry out the interrogation; a tape recorder, reporters, other possibilities had been abandoned while work continued on the piece. When I asked if the new play owed any debt to Milton, Chaikin quizzically pondered the possibility, wondering if Shepard had some such connection in mind. The "Angel's Monologue" from *The War in Heaven* subsequently appeared in the tenth anniversary edition of the *Performing Arts Journal*. Rick Harris produced it for radio in October 1984, and it was first broadcast over WBAI in January 1985.

On the set of *Country*, Shepard told an interviewer that his first love was the stage, and that *Country* would be his last film. Since then, his screenplay *Paris, Texas* has won the Palme d'Or at the 1984 Cannes Film Festival. In collaboration with the gifted German film director Wim Wenders, Shepard has produced a screenplay that movingly recounts the story of Travis Henderson, an ordinary American man who is first seen striding determinedly across the desert (filmed at Devil's Graveyard, Big Bend, Texas), a landscape to which he assuredly will return after reuniting his wife and son. *Paris, Texas* is surely Shepard's best work in film to date. It is a film that clearly belongs to a man whose heart is with the stage; like Shepard's earlier plays, *Paris, Texas* depends for its powerful effects on a series of images rapidly juxtaposed with minimal dialogue to supplement his photographic collage. In February 1984, Shepard was one of four artists who received a Brandeis Creative Arts Award recognizing lifetime achievement in the arts.

In November of 1985, Shepard's play *A Lie of the Mind* premiered at New York's Promenade Theatre, adding a fifth play to the collection of domestic dramas. *A Lie of the Mind* was named outstanding new play of the 1985-86 New York theatre season by the Drama Desk. A few weeks later, the film version of *Fool for Love* was released. Perhaps the lure of the screen has captured Shepard at last, but the soul of a playwright rests securely in the work of Sam Shepard, on stage or screen.

NOTES

1. Sam Shepard, "Metaphors, Mad Dogs, and Old Time Cowboys," an interview with Kenneth Chubb *et al.*, *Theatre Quarterly*, 4, No. 15 (1974), p. 3.

2. Sam Shepard, *Hawk Moon* (New York: Performing Arts Journal Press, 1981), p. 41.

3. Shepard, *Theatre Quarterly*, p. 3.

4. *Ibid.*

5. Sam Shepard, "Autobiography," *News of the American Place Theatre*, 3, No. 3 (April 1971), p. 1.

6. Sam Shepard, as quoted by Robert Goldberg, "Sam Shepard, American Original," *Playboy*, V. 31, March 1984, p. 191.

7. *Ibid.*

8. Elenore Lester, "In the Parish Hall, the Hippies Go Ape," *New York Times*, 26 March 1967, sec. 2, p. 1.

9. Shepard, *Theatre Quarterly*, p. 5.

10. *Ibid.*

11. Ralph Cook, quoted by Michael Vermuelen in "Sam Shepard, Yes, Yes, Yes," *Esquire* February 1980, p. 80.

12. Michael Smith, "Theatre: *Cowboys* and *The Rock Garden*," *The Village Voice*, 22 October 1964, p. 13.

13. *Ibid.*

14. Michael Smith, rev. of *Chicago*, by Sam Shepard, *The Village Voice*, 13 May 1965, p. 17.

15. Edward Albee, rev. of *Icarus' Mother*, by Sam Shepard, *The Village Voice*, 25 November 1965, p. 19.

16. Shepard, *Theatre Quarterly*, p. 5.

17. Sam Shepard, as quoted by Stephen Fay, "The Silent Type," *Vogue*, V. 213, February 1985, p. 17.

18. Stanley Kauffmann, "Last 3 Plays of '6 From La Mama' Offered at the Martinique," rev. of *Chicago* by Sam Shepard, *New York Times*, 13 April 1966, sec. 2, p. 36.

19. Penelope Gilliatt, rev. of *Brand X*, CMB, *The New Yorker*, 46 (1970), pp. 115–116.

20. Irving Wardle, rev. of *Red Cross*, by Sam Shepard, *The Times*, 3 April 1970, p. 13.

21. Clive Barnes, rev. of *The Tooth of Crime*, by Sam Shepard, *New York Times*, 12 November 1972, sec. 4, p. 77.

22. Clive Barnes, "Max Ernst, Looking Backwards," *The Times*, 1 March 1975, sec. 1, p. 7.

23. Robert Palmer, "A Rock Tour Recalled," *New York Times*, 17 September 1977, sec. 1, p. 21.

24. Stanley Kauffmann, rev. of *Days of Heaven* by Terence Malick, Paramount, 1978, *The New Republic*, 16 September 1978, p. 17.

25. Sam Shepard, quoted by Mel Gussow, rev. of *Savage/Love* by Sam Shepard, *New York Times*, 16 November 1979, sec. 1, p. 6.

26. Richard Corliss, rev. of *Resurrection*, by Lewis John Carlino, Universal, 1980, *Time*, 3 November 1980, p. 116.

27. Robert Coe, "The Saga of Sam Shepard," *New York Times Magazine*, 130, 23 November 1980, p. 58.

28. David Ansen, "The Reluctant Saint," *Newsweek*, 96, November 17, 1980, pp. 117–118.

29. *Ibid*. p. 117.

30. *Ibid*.

31. Michiko Kakutani, "Myths, Dreams, Realities—Sam Shepard's America," *New York Times*, 29 January 1982, sec. 2, p. 26.

32. A conversation with the author and Joseph Chaikin at the Contemporary Arts Center, New Orleans, Louisiana, March 17, 1984.

APPENDIX II

SHEPARD IN PRINT AND PRODUCTION

Every effort has been made to give the exact date of opening productions. For some plays that information has been inaccessible.

Action in *Sam Shepard: Fool for Love and Other Plays* (New York: Bantam Books, 1984).
  First Production: 16 September 1974, Theatre Upstairs at the Royal Court, London.
  American Premiere: 4 April 1975, the American Place Theatre, New York City.

Angel City in *Sam Shepard: Angel City and Other Plays* (New York: Urizen Press, 1976).*
  Angel City also reprinted in *Fool for Love and Other Plays*.
  First Production: 2 July 1976, the Magic Theatre, San Francisco.

Back Bog Beast Bait in *The Unseen Hand and Other Plays* (New York: Urizen Press, 1981), and in the Bantam ed. of *The Unseen Hand and Other Plays*.
  First Production: 29 April 1971, the American Place Theatre, New York City.

Blue Bitch (unpublished)
  Broadcast by the BBC in spring 1973.

Buried Child in *Sam Shepard: Buried Child, Seduced, Suicide in B♭* (New York: Urizen Press, 1981). Reprinted in *Sam Shepard: Seven Plays* (New York: Bantam Books, 1984).
  First Production: 27 June 1978, the Magic Theatre, San Francisco.

Chicago in *Chicago and Other Plays* (New York: Urizen Press, 1967). Reprinted in *The Unseen Hand and Other Plays* (Bantam).

*Applause Theatre Book Publishers redistributed the Urizen collections in 1984.

First Production: 16 April 1965, Theatre Genesis, St. Mark's Church in-the-Bouwerie, New York City.

Cowboy Mouth in *Mad Dog Blues and Other Plays* (New York: Winter House L.T.D., 1972). Reprinted in *Fool for Love and Other Plays*.
First Production: 12 April 1971, Traverse Theatre, Edinburgh.
American Premiere: 29 April 1971, the American Place Theatre, New York City.

Cowboys (unpublished)
First Production: 10 October 1964, Theatre Genesis, New York City.

Cowboys #2 in *Mad Dog Blues and Other Plays*. Reprinted in *Angel City and Other Plays*, and in *The Unseen Hand and Other Plays* (Bantam).
First Production: 12 August 1967, Old Reliable Theatre, New York City.
In November 1967 produced by the Mark Taper Forum, Los Angeles.

Curse of the Starving Class in *Angel City and Other Plays*. Reprinted in *Sam Shepard: Seven Plays*.
First Production: April 1977, Royal Court Theatre, London.
American Premiere: 2 March 1978, the New York Shakespeare Festival, New York City.

Dog (unpublished)
First Production: 10 February 1965, La Mama Experimental Theatre Club, New York City.

Fool for Love in *Fool for Love and Other Plays* and *Fool for Love* (San Francisco: City Lights Books, 1983).
First Production: 8 February 1983, the Magic Theatre, San Francisco.

Forensic and the Navigators in *The Unseen Hand and Other Plays*.
First Production: 29 December 1967, Theatre Genesis, New York City.

4-H Club in *The Unseen Hand and Other Plays*.
First Production: 1965, Cherry Lane Theatre, New York City.

Fourteen Hundred Thousand in *Chicago and Other Plays*, and in *The Unseen Hand and Other Plays*.
First Production: 1966, Firehouse Theatre, Minneapolis.
Subsequently produced on National Educational Television.

Geography of a Horse Dreamer in *Sam Shepard: Four Two-Act Plays* (New York: 1980). Reprinted in *Fool for Love and Other Plays*.
First Production: 2 February 1974, Theatre Upstairs at the Royal Court, London.

The Holy Ghostly in *The Unseen Hand and Other Plays.*
    First Production: By the New Troupe branch of La Mama under
    the direction of Tom O'Horgan on the 1969 European and
    American college tour.
Icarus's Mother in *Chicago and Other Plays,* and in *The Unseen Hand and
    Other Plays.*
    First Production: 16 November 1965, Caffe Cino, New York City.
Inacoma (unpublished)
    First Production: 18 March 1977, the Magic Theatre, San Fran-
    cisco.
Jacaranda (unpublished)
    Libretto for Daniel Nagrin, produced May 1979 by Playhouse 46
    in St. Clement's Church, New York City.
Killer's Head in *Angel City and Other Plays,* and in *The Unseen Hand and
    Other Plays.*
    First Production: 4 April 1975, the American Place Theatre, New
    York City.
La Turista in *Sam Shepard: Four Two-Act Plays* (New York: Urizen Press,
    1980), and in *Seven Plays.*
    First Production: 4 March 1967, the American Place Theatre, New
    York City.
A Lie of the Mind (unpublished)
    First Production: 22 November 1985, Promenade Theatre, New
    York City.
Little Ocean (unpublished)
    First Production: 25 March 1974, Hampstead Theatre Club,
    London.
The Mad Dog Blues in *Mad Dog Blues and Other Plays.* Reprinted in *Angel
    City and Other Plays,* and in *The Unseen Hand and Other Plays.*
    First Production: 4 March 1971, Theatre Genesis, New York City.
Melodrama Play in *Chicago and Other Plays.* Reprinted in *Fool for Love
    and Other Plays.*
    First Production: 18 May 1967, La Mama Experimental Theatre
    Club, New York City.
Operation Sidewinder in *The Unseen Hand and Other Plays.*
    First Production: 12 March 1970, Repertory Theatre of Lincoln
    Center, New York City.
Red Cross in *Chicago and Other Plays,* and in *The Unseen Hand and Other
    Plays.*
    First Production: January 1966, the Judson Poet's Theatre, New
    York City.
The Rock Garden in *Mad Dog Blues and Other Plays.* Reprinted in *Angel*

City and Other Plays, and in *The Unseen Hand and Other Plays*.
First Production: 10 October 1964, Theatre Genesis, New York
City.
The final scene of *The Rock Garden* was performed as part of the
revue, *Oh! Calcutta*, which opened on June 17, 1969.

Rocking Chair (unpublished)
First Production: 10 February 1965, La Mama Experimental Theatre Club, New York City.

The Sad Lament of Pecos Bill on the Eve of Killing His Wife in *Fool for Love
and The Sad Lament of Pecos Bill* (San Francisco: City Lights, 1983).
First Production: September 1983, La Mama Experimental Theatre Club, New York City.

Savage/Love (with Joseph Chaikin) in *Sam Shepard: Seven Plays*.
First Production: November 1979, the Public Theater, New York
City.

Seduced in *Buried Child, Seduced, and Suicide in B♭*. Reprinted in *Fool for
Love and Other Plays*.
First Production: February 1979, the American Place Theatre,
New York City.

Shaved Splits in *The Unseen Hand and Other Plays*. (Urizen ed. only)
First Production: 20 July 1970, Cafe La Mama, New York City.

Suicide in B♭ in *Buried Child, Seduced and Suicide in B♭*. Reprinted in *Fool
for Love and Other Plays*.
First Production: 15 October 1976, Yale Repertory Theatre, New
Haven, Connecticut.

Superstitions (unpublished)
First Production: September 1983, La Mama Experimental Theatre Club, New York City.

Tongues (with Joseph Chaikin) in *Sam Shepard: Seven Plays*.
First Production: 1978, the Magic Theatre, San Francisco.

The Tooth of Crime in *Four Two-Act Plays*. Reprinted in *Sam Shepard:
Seven Plays*.
First Production: 17 July 1972, the Open Space, London.
American Premiere: 11 November 1972, the McCarter Theater,
Princeton, New Jersey.

True West in *Sam Shepard: Seven Plays*.
First Production: 10 July 1980, the Magic Theatre, San Francisco.

The Unseen Hand in *The Unseen Hand and Other Plays*.
First Production: 26 December 1969, La Mama Experimental
Theatre Club, New York City.

Up to Thursday (unpublished)

First Production: 10 February 1965, Cherry Lane Theatre, New York City.

Bantam Books released a new edition of Shepard plays in 1986: *Sam Shepard: The Unseen Hand and Other Plays* (New York: Bantam Books, 1986). The collection includes: *The Unseen Hand, The Rock Garden, Chicago, Icarus's Mother, 4-H Club, Fourteen Hundred Thousand, Red Cross, Cowboys #2, Forensic and the Navigators, The Holy Ghostly, Operation Sidewinder, The Mad Dog Blues, Back Bog Beast Bait,* and *Killer's Head.*

The War in Heaven (Angel's Monologue) with Joseph Chaikin in *Performing Arts Journal*, tenth anniversary edition, 2627, Vol. ix, 2 and 3, pp. 249–262.

Screenplays:

Fool for Love, written by Sam Shepard, directed by Robert Altman, released December 6, 1985.

Paris, Texas, written by Sam Shepard, adaptation by L. M. Kit Carson, directed by Wim Wenders (Berlin: Road Movies, 1984).

Poetry and Prose:

Hawk Moon (New York: Performing Arts Journal Publications, 1981).

Motel Chronicles (San Francisco: City Lights, 1982).

The Rolling Thunder Logbook (New York: Viking Press, 1977).

BIBLIOGRAPHY OF CRITICAL WORKS

Ansen, David. "The Reluctant Saint: The Reluctant Star." *Newsweek*, 96, 17 November 1980, pp. 117–118.

Auerbach, Doris. *Sam Shepard, Arthur Kopit, and the Off-Broadway Theater*. Boston: Twayne Publishers, 1982.

Bachman, Charles R. "Defusion of Menace in the Plays of Sam Shepard." *Modern Drama*, 19, No. 4 (Dec. 1976), 405–415.

Barnes, Clive. "The Theater: Sam Shepard's *The Tooth of Crime*." *New York Times*, 12 November 1972, sec. 4, p. 77.

Bigsby, C. W. E. *et al.* "Theatre Checklist No. 3, Sam Shepard." *Theatrefacts*, 3 (Aug.–Oct. 1974), 3–11.

Blau, Herbert. "The American Dream in American Gothic: The Plays of Sam Shepard and Adrienne Kennedy." *Modern Drama*, 27, No. 4 (Dec. 1984), 520–539.

Boyd, Blanche McCrary. "Sam Shepard—Playwright, Actor, Man in Love." *Cosmopolitan*, 198, January 1985, pp. 62–66.

Brustein, Robert. "Love from Two Sides of the Ocean." *The New Republic*, 188, 27 June 1983, pp. 24–25.

Chubb, Kenneth. "Fruitful Difficulties of Directing Shepard." *Theatre Quarterly*, 4, No. 15 (Aug.–Oct. 1974), 17–26.

Coe, Robert. "The Saga of Sam Shepard." *New York Times Magazine*, 130, 23 November 1980, p. 56 (8).

Cohn, Ruby. *New American Dramatists: 1960–1980*. New York: Grove Press, 1982.

Croyden, Margaret. "The Playwright Vanishes: Reflections on Today's Theater." *New York Times*, 20 June 1982, sec. 2, pp. 1 and 33.

Davis, Richard A. " 'Get Up Outa' Your Homemade Beds': The Plays of Sam Shepard." *Players*, 47 (Oct./Nov. 1971), 12–19.

Eder, Richard. "Sam Shepard's Obsession is America." *New York Times*, 4 March 1979, sec. 2, p. 1.

Falk, Florence. "The Role of Performance in Sam Shepard's Plays." *Theatre Journal*, 33, No. 2 (May 1981), 182–198.

Fay, Stephen. "the silent type." *Vogue*, 175, No. 4 (February 1985), 213–218.

Feingold, Michael. "Sam Shepard, Part-time Shaman." *The Village Voice*, 4 April 1977, pp. 72 and 75.

Freedman, Samuel. "Sam Shepard and the Mythic Family." *New York Times*, 1 December 1985, sec. 2, pp. 1 and 20.

Funke, Lewis. "Singing the Rialto Blues." *New York Times*, 5 March 1967, sec. 2, p. 5.

Ganz, Arthur. *Realms of the Self: Variations on a Theme in Modern Drama*. New York: New York University Press, 1980.

Glore, John. "The Canonization of Mojo Rootforce: Sam Shepard Live at the Pantheon." *Theater*, 12, No. 3 (Sum./Fall 1981), 53–65.

Goldberg, Robert. "Sam Shepard, American Original." *Playboy*, 31, March 1984, pp. 90, 112, 192–193.

Gussow, Mel. "The Deeply American Roots of Sam Shepard's Plays." *New York Times*, 2 January 1979, sec. 2, p. 1.

Gussow, Mel. "Intimate Monologues That Speak to the Mind and the Heart." *New York Times*, 19 December 1979, sec. 1, p. 3, col. 1.

Hamill, Pete. "The New American Hero." *New York*, 5 December 1983, pp. 75–102.

Homan, Richard L. "American Playwrights in the 1970's: Rabe and Shepard." *Critical Quarterly*, 24, No. 1 (Spring 1982), 73–82.

Hughes, Catherine. *American Playwrights, 1945–1975*. London: Pitman Press, 1976.

Jackson, Esther M. "American Theatre in the Sixties." *Players*, 48 (Summer 1973), 236–249.

Kakutani, Michiko. "Myths, Dreams, Realities—Sam Shepard's America." *New York Times*, 29 January 1984, sec. 2, pp. 1 and 26–28.

Kauffmann, Stanley. "True to Life, True to Film." *The New Republic*, 189, 14 November 1982, pp. 24–26.

Kerr, Walter. "Where Has Sam Shepard Led His Audience?" *New York Times*, 5 June 1983, sec. 2, pp. 1 and 16.

Kihss, Peter. "Shepard Takes Pulitzer for Drama." *New York Times*, 17 April 1979, sec. 1, p. 1

Kleb, William. "Sam Shepard's *Inacoma* at the Magic Theatre." *Theater*, 9 (Fall 1977), 59–64.

Kleb, William. "Shepard and Chaikin Speaking in *Tongues*." *Theater*, 10, No. 1 (Fall 1978), 66–69.

Kleb, William. "The Sunshine Muse: Creating the California Play-wright." *The Performing Arts Journal*, 4, No. 3 (1980), 60–71.

Kopkind, Andrew. "Countrification." *The Nation*, 239, 27 October 1984, pp. 425–426.

Kramer, Mimi. "In Search of the Good Shepard." *The New Criterion*, 2, No. 2 (Oct. 1983), 51–57.

Kroll, Jack. "Who's That Tall, Dark Stranger?" *Newsweek*, 11 November 1985, pp. 68–74.

Lahr, John. *Up Against the Fourth Wall: Essays on Modern Theater*. New York: Grove Press, 1968.

Lewis, Allan. *American Plays and Playwrights of the Contemporary Theatre*. New York: Crown Pub., 1970.

Lion, John. "Rock 'n Roll Jesus with a Cowboy Mouth: Sam Shepard is the Inkblot of the '80s." *American Theatre*, 1, No. 1 (April 1984), 4–13.

Madden, David. "The Theatre of Assault: Four Off-Off-Broadway Plays." *The Massachusetts Review*, 8, No. 4 (1967), 713–725.

Malpede, Karen, ed. *Three Works by the Open Theatre*. New York: Drama Book Specialists, 1974.

Marranca, Bonnie, ed. *American Dreams: The Imagination of Sam Shepard*. New York: Performing Arts Journal Press, 1981.

Marranca, Bonnie and Gautam Dasgupta, eds. *American Playwrights: A Critical Survey*. Vol. 1. New York: Drama Book Specialists, 1981.

Mazzocco, Robert. "Sam Shepard's Big Roundup." *The New York Review of Books*, 32, No. 8, 9 May 1985, pp. 21–27.

McCarthy, Gerry. " 'Acting It Out': Sam Shepard's *Action*." *Modern Drama*, 24, No. 1 (March 1981), 1–12.

Mottram, Ron. *Inner Landscapes: The Theater of Sam Shepard*. Columbia, Mo.: University of Missouri Press, 1984.

Nightingale, Benedict. "Even Minimal Shepard is Food for Thought." *New York Times*, 25 September 1983, sec. 2, pp. 5 and 26.

Oppenheim, Irene and Victor Fascio. "The Most Promising Playwright in America Today is Sam Shepard." *The Village Voice*, 27 October 1975, pp. 80–82.

Orbison, Tucker. "Mythic Levels in Sam Shepard's *True West*." *Modern Drama*, 27, No. 4 (Dec. 1984), 506–519.

Pasolli, Robert. "The New Playwrights' Scene of the Sixties: Jerome Max is Alive and Well and Living in Rome . . . " *Tulane Drama Review*, 13, No. 1 (Fall 1968), 150–168.

Peachment, Chris. "The Time Out Interview." *Time Out*, London, August 23–29, 1984, No. 731.

Powe, Bruce W. "*The Tooth of Crime*: Sam Shepard's Way with Music." *Modern Drama*, 24, No. 1 (March 1981), 39–46.

Rich, Frank. "Stage: Shepard's *True West*." *New York Times*, 24 December 1980, sec. 1, p. 9.

Rosen, Carol. "Sam Shepard's *Angel City*: A Movie for the Stage." *Modern Drama*, 22, No. 1 (March 1979), 39–46.

Savran, David. "Sam Shepard's Conceptual Prison: *Action* and the *Unseen Hand*." *Theatre Journal*, 36, No. 1 (March 1984), 57–74.

Shepard, Sam. "American Experimental Theatre Then and Now." *Performing Arts Journal*, 2, No. 2 (Fall 1977), 13–14.

Shepard, Sam. "Autobiography." *News of the American Place Theatre*, 3, No. 3 (April 1971), 1–3.

Shepard, Sam. "Metaphors, Mad Dogs and Old-Time Cowboys." *Theatre Quarterly*, 4, No. 15 (Aug.–Oct. 1974), 3–16.

Shepard, Sam. "Visualization, Language, and the Inner Library." *Drama Review*, 21, No. 4 (Dec. 1977), 49–58.

Shewey, Don. *Sam Shepard*. New York: Dell Publishing Co., 1985.

Simon, John. "Soft Centers." *New York*, 16, 13 June 1983, pp. 76–77.

Simon, John. "Theater Chronicle: Kopit, Norman, and Shepard." *Hudson Review*, 32 (Spring 1979), 77–88.

Smith, Michael. "Theatre: *Cowboys* and *The Rock Garden*." *The Village Voice*, 22 October 1964, p. 13.

Smith, Michael, ed. *More Plays from Off-Off-Broadway*. New York: The Bobbs-Merrill Co., 1972.

Smith, Michael and Nick Orzel, eds. *Eight Plays from Off-Off-Broadway*. New York: The Bobbs-Merrill Co., 1966.

Smith, Patti. "Sam Shepard: Nine Random Years (7 + 2)." In *Sam Shepard: Mad Dog Blues and Other Plays*. New York: Winter House, 1972.

Thomson, David. "Shepard." *Film Comment*, 19 (Dec. 1983), 49–56.

Weales, Gerald. "American Theater Watch, 1979–1980." *Georgia Review*, 34 (1980), 497–508.

Wetzsteon, Ross. "Sam Shepard: Escape Artist." *Partisan Review*, 49, No. 2 (1982), 253–261.

Wetzsteon, Ross. "A Season for All Seasons." *The Village Voice*, 6 June 1977, p. 93.

Zinman, Toby Silverman. "Shepard Suite." *American Theatre*, 1, No. 8 (Dec. 1984), 15–17.

INDEX

About the Author

LYNDA HART is an Assistant Professor of English at Xavier University in Cincinnati where she teaches modern and contemporary drama and Shakespeare. She has articles forthcoming on Marsha Norman, Megan Terry, and Wendy Kesselman, and she is currently working on a collection of critical essays on feminist playwrights.